I Believe That

_____

Can
Get It Together!!

Mamie McCullough
Jeremiah 33:3

GET IT TOGETHER

AND REMEMBER WHERE YOU PUT IT

by

Mamie McCullough

Second Printing

Get It Together
And Remember Where You Put It
ISBN 1-56292-380-3
Copyright © 1997 by Mamie McCullough & Associates
PMB 372
305 Spring Creek Village
Dallas, Texas 75248

In Gratitude

This book is dedicated to the thousands of my Angel Friends across this country. Each of you has touched my life in some special, positive way and thus has provided needed encouragement and impetus for my writing this book.

Some of you gave a smile...

Some of you gave a hug...

Some of you gave a letter...

Some of you gave an idea...

Some of you gave a prayer...

Some of you gave your all...

Thanks to each of you...know that *I love you*.

Mamie

CONTENTS

FOREWORD

I've always believed you should surround yourself with vibrant, successful people who are full of hope and vision. Mamie McCullough is such an individual, and I'm privileged to know her as a friend. But for those of you who cannot rub shoulders with Mamie, *Get It Together and Remember Where You Put It* offers a not-to-be-missed opportunity of friendship, support, and inspiration.

This book shows people how to cultivate their talents, live with enthusiasm, and visualize success. This is not another tome on organizational theory; instead, it's a blueprint for getting our lives together...for believing in ourselves...and for achieving effective, satisfying lives.

Mamie speaks from the crucible of experience. Born and raised in poverty with eight brothers and sisters, Mamie could have yielded to a life of despair. But today she tours the country exhorting others to be the best that they can be.

As I read the manuscript for this book, I kept thinking of a world of people who would be uplifted by Mamie's words. And the words of another precious friend (and mentor) came to mind. The late Mary C. Crowley often said, "The whole world needs a dose of hope." How true! And here it is — in a book with a healing dose of hope for a crying world that wants desperately to be loved and encouraged.

I challenge any one of you who has lost hope — or the joy of living, or the realization that God is on your side, or the childlike quality of dreaming big dreams — to spend time learning about yourself and the "its" of your life through this dramatically written book. I can promise you that this book will be a step to becoming all God wants you to be.

God bless you,

Barbara Hammond
Senior Vice President and National Sales Manager
Home Interiors & Gifts, Inc.

A Word From Mamie

A few of my friends who knew I was writing this book asked me to explain the title, *Get It Together and Remember Where You Put It.* I told them the "it" stood for "your life." And surely everyone would like to be a "together" person, one who has all aspects of his or her life pulling smoothly and steadily ahead in a positive direction. For me, the "remember where you put it" part may be the real challenge, though. After I finally get things together, they don't always *stay* together where they can do the most good. I forget, so to speak, to keep all my ducks in a row. When I remember where I put things, life proceeds smoothly. That is what I hope this book will assist you to do: get your life together and keep it on track, running smoothly and efficiently in order for you to be all you can be.

Most of my life to date has been spent "getting it together." That took so long that I am now into that time zone where remembering where I put it is starting to pose a real problem. I laughingly tell my audiences that I'm at the stage of my life where it is not downhill...but upkeep. Many of you must know what I mean.

We have to keep working with and improving all the various areas of our lives. To stay clean on the outside, we have to take a bath every day. The same principle applies to keeping our life "together" on the inside — we have to keep up a persistent maintenance program in order to remember where we put it.

Let me provide a little background on how some of the ideas that helped me get my life together evolved to the point where I want to share them with you. Go back with me to Dallas in 1979, when I went to work for Zig Ziglar. Prior to that time, the thought of speaking before large groups of people had never entered my mind. I had been a teacher and a principal at a large high school in Georgia, but had done no public speaking. My new job was to work with schools and appear before small groups of teachers promoting the "I CAN" curriculum that I had written

9

based on Zig's book, *See You at the Top*. Most likely I would have decided the Lord wanted me to stay in Georgia, if I had known that traveling and speaking were to be an important part of introducing the "I CAN" philosophy to schools. Almost immediately, more schools than I expected began to ask me to come and explain the curriculum that I had written and how it was designed to motivate, improve relationships, set goals, and improve the self-image of students and teachers. It was with considerable trepidation that I started to do more traveling, speaking first to small groups and then gradually to increasingly bigger audiences.

At first I did not know how much of a fee to charge. In fact, I probably would have even paid for the privilege of speaking at some schools if they had pressed the point. Educators were the only people I spoke to back then, and my fee was around two hundred dollars. My speech at that time consisted of explaining the "I CAN" curriculum, answering questions, and telling some of Zig's stories. I even sold his books and autographed them. Then an unexpected event occurred that gave my career a huge lift and my message a critical change.

It was late on a Thursday afternoon in March, 1980, and for some reason I had delayed leaving the office. My phone rang. The call was from Dr. Mary Allen, the in-service coordinator of Cameron University in Lawton, Oklahoma. She said, "Mamie, I hope you will not be insulted. You were one of our top choices to come to our school for a teacher in-service training program; however, the committee chose Dr. Joyce Brothers."

I could understand that, of course, so I said, "Why then are you calling me?"

She said, "Well, we did contract with Dr. Brothers to make the speech, but she called today to tell me she will be unable to come because she has developed laryngitis. The speech is tomorrow and we wondered if at this late date you could come and take her place?"

My answer was evasive, because I certainly did not feel qualified to replace Joyce Brothers. But somehow, "Well, yes" came out of my mouth.

Dr. Allen continued, "And Mamie, I need to tell you that we only have fifteen hundred dollars to pay you and that includes expenses. Would that be all right?"

Understand that I was charging somewhere between zero and two hundred dollars and had never even heard a fifteen-hundred-dollar speech — much less made one. In attempting to respond to this second shocking statement, I again let the word "yes" slip from my lips.

At that point I knew we were both stuck, and I began feeling sorry for both of us. Here Dr. Allen was grossly overpaying someone who could not adequately replace an ailing Joyce Brothers, and I had to find a fifteen-hundred-dollar speech and had absolutely no clue where to look. I knew I was in trouble, and Dr. Allen probably wondered if she might have solved one problem, only to create another.

That evening and night I worried and stewed, trying to decide what I would say and, of course, what I would wear. The next morning I put on my "Nelly New" suit (bought at my favorite resale shop) and headed for the airport. My ticket cost seventy-seven dollars (some things we never forget), and I was off to Lawton, still with no speech — a lot of notes and ideas, but no speech.

It was a perfect spring day as we leveled off at cruising altitude for the short flight to Tulsa. Beautiful, puffy white clouds stretched to the horizon as I started to pray, "Lord, You know I never dreamed I would be in this situation. God, I'm asking You to give me a fifteen-hundred-dollar speech, because I have no idea of what to say and people are counting on me."

I continued to pray and a few moments later a feeling of peace and confidence came over me. Something to my right caught my attention, and as I turned in that direction the morning sun moved above the clouds and shone brightly through the plane's windows. The topic for my speech was now clear in my mind. It was as if the Lord was telling me, *Mamie, tell your story. Just tell your story.*

Since I had left my home in Dixie, Georgia, at age twenty, I had never told anyone the story of how I was raised and the trials and tribulations I had faced. Frankly, I was embarrassed about having been so poor as a child and about some of the things that had happened to me then and later as an adult. Why should this audience or any other be interested in a poor Georgia girl's struggle against long odds to "be better"? I did not know the answer to that question, but I did know the answer to my prayer was very clear and specific. *Just tell your story!*

So I made some new notes, and that day I told my story — what had happened to me and what I had learned from my experiences. Many of you know that my story bears little resemblance to a fairy tale. But I told it, and it must have been the right thing to do because I received a standing ovation when I finished.

A few weeks later at one of our seminars for teachers, a lady came up to me and said, "Mamie, you tell Mr. Ziglar's stories beautifully; but I believe you have some stories of your own, and I want to encourage you to tell them." So that was the second validation that I should be using more of my own personal illustrations. My story became the first of what would later comprise two primary parts of my presentations. The other part is the material you will read on these pages.

The ten years following that speech in Lawton have seen a dramatic increase in the use of the "I CAN" curriculum in schools across the nation. Our best estimate is that more than five million students have been exposed to the "I CAN" philosophy of life through the curriculum that I first started writing in 1974.

In 1987, my story was published with the title, *I Can. You Can Too!* The book's basic idea is that it is not where you start, but where you finish that counts. And it's not what happens to you, but what you do with what happens to you that is important. That book, which is now in its fourth printing, has helped many people believe that if Mamie McCullough could persevere and make it — then so could they!

A special feature of *I Can. You Can Too!* is the spelling I used for the word *be* — *bee*. In the book you are now reading, you will occasionally encounter that same spelling. I use it in order to remind you and me to *bee* all that God wants and allows us to *bee*. The inspiration came from the bumblebee, a symbol of perseverance and hard work. Though it has been determined by the scientist that the bumblebee is aerodynamically unable to fly, he is unable to read what they have written about him, so he flies anyway. Through God, all things are possible.

My speaking engagements have changed and expanded over the years, with church and business audiences added to the education groups. The size of my audiences has also increased. Now I often speak to groups numbering in the thousands, and on two occasions I have spoken to more than twenty thousand. Shyness, like anything else, can be overcome.

The second part of my presentations for these educators, business groups, and churches consists of the techniques and strategies that, when practiced, can dramatically improve the quality of our lives. The ideas I share have helped me in good times, but, more particularly, they have permitted me to come safely through the very difficult times in my life. When we personally package these ideas together with our desires to be better, they become our plan to get and keep our lives together and headed in the right direction.

We all need a well-thought-out, proven plan that will harness our energies, talents, and desires. *Get It Together and Remember Where You Put It* is my attempt to share ideas, techniques, and strategies for improving your life, no matter how impossible your circumstances may seem. From these resources, I firmly believe you will be able to construct a proven plan of action that will permit you to turn your desire for a better life into positive results.

In order for us to reach any goal, three basic things are necessary:

1. Strong desire.

2. A valid plan consisting of strategies and techniques.

3. Action — implementation of the plan.

My goal is to help you improve the quality of your life, starting today and starting from where you are right now. I want you to be aware of and to understand some insights that I *know* will help you as they have helped me.

You cannot feel any worse than I have felt in the past. You cannot feel any better than I feel today. Many of the weights that I carried for so long have now been lifted from my shoulders. Any extra weights that you carry also need to be lifted. The ideas presented in the following pages are my best effort to provide you with guidance and assistance so that you can remove some of the weights that hold you back. Remember — you are important. You have great potential. You are special. *I believe in you!*

I CAN AND YOU CAN TOO!

I can and you can too!

Is my strong belief about the future for you.

Start where you are — and go where you want to go

With knowledge and action — it's not who you know.

I'll encourage you — you help others — it's God's will.

To overcome together — hand in hand — is the ultimate thrill.

Remember I'm with you as you strive to succeed;

My prayer and belief are that God will fill your every need!

HEARTITUDE

I Believe
in

You!

The "Heartitude" on the preceding page is the first of several that you will find throughout this book. Heartitudes are short written or verbal encouragements from the heart — tools that I have included to help you make your life better.

You Can Make "It" Better

One of my strongest convictions is that you can make your life better — no matter what your situation is today! How I hope things are going great for you. I hope your situation is strong and improving, with all areas of your life in a strong up trend. However, if your world is a little unsettled or if times are extremely difficult, don't despair. You can make it better! **Wherever you are today in your life, this is what I believe about your ability — and thus your future:**

♥ • ♥ • ♥ • ♥ • ♥

HEARTITUDE

No matter what you've done — I believe in you

No matter what's happened to you — I believe in you

No matter what people say — I believe in you

No matter if you are rich or poor — I believe in you

I Believe

in

No matter what your age or size — I believe in you

No matter your IQ — I believe in you

You!

No matter where you live — I believe in you

No matter your position or lack of one — I believe in you

No matter, no matter, no matter —

♥ • ♥ • ♥ • ♥ • ♥

I believe in you!!

Dear reader, in case there is still any doubt, you are stuck with my believing in you. Just call it unconditional belief. I can believe in whatever or whomever I choose, and I choose to believe in *you*. Something else you need to know up front is that I am a "heart" speaker and writer and not a "head" speaker and writer. There is not necessarily a conflict between the two, but I always lead from my heart and hope the words later check out with my head. My mother used to say, "Mamie, if you know it's right in your heart — do it." I have added "and say it" to her admonition. So I write as I speak...from my heart to your heart.

WE ALL WANT TO BE BETTER

One of the strongest desires of my life has always been to be better. It started in Dixie, Georgia, when I was poor, fatherless, and just trying to make it through one more day. There were so many things I did not have, did not know, and never expected to accomplish that I just put everything I dreamed of for myself into the generalized "be better" category. I wanted to be better, but had no idea how to do it. Also, I never expected it to happen. All I could do was work and dream. As poor as we were, the work was not optional, and dreaming was just about all the entertainment we could afford.

I later found out that everyone wants to be better. Everyone. Even those who are already "better" want to be better still. Even those who seem like they could not possibly improve want to be better.

All of us have different areas of our lives that we want to improve and fix up; we all want progress in some direction. This desire is always with us, although some want it more than others. Intensity varies among people. I hope your intensity and desire levels are high because that helps.

Too often, we are not permitted stable conditions in which to work on our desire to be better. Major difficulties and problems arise that demand total concentration and effort if we are to handle them successfully. Problems are really a quite natural part of life. We just need to avoid those we can and learn to solve the rest.

Let me say here that I believe you can overcome any difficulty you are faced with at this moment or will be faced with in the future. This strong belief is based on my own personal experience and on careful observation of others over a long period of time.

Speaking of a long period of time, there's something we may as well get out of the way before we go any farther. I'll just go ahead and tell you my age — I'm fifty-something! Two years ago I was forty-something, and I had been that age ever since I was thirty-something.

When I turned fifty, Mike Vander Werf, a young man who was helping me with my speaking engagements at the time, asked me if I planned to tell my age. I assured him that I certainly was, because there must be no mistake...with people thinking that I'm thirty but looking fifty.

In any case, I've had a lot of years both to observe and experience problems of all types, to see how we respond to them, and duly note the results. I've seen what works and what doesn't, what helps us and what hurts us, and I've reached what I believe are valid conclusions.

Although I am always optimistic, I am not a "Pollyanna" about the condition of this road of life we all travel. There are numerous tough spots and many potholes of varying sizes on this road. We must learn to avoid as many dangerous areas as possible, while also preparing for those unavoidable potholes. Then we must absorb the shock and press on to our destination.

MY TRUE TALENT

In my work, I meet a lot of different people with talents in many areas. I've met and talked with all kinds of experts, people who know their particular field of endeavor as well as anyone else in the world. Earlier in my life I would have felt nervous, inferior, and out of my depth as a result of being around such people. No longer. I now feel good about myself and what I'm doing. And I recognize that I am just as much an expert in my field as they are in theirs. Not in speaking and writing, let me hasten to add — that's not the field in which I am claiming expertise. My hard-earned talent is overcoming difficulties — hitting life's potholes, taking the jolt, regrouping, and proceeding on down the road.

Here is just a partial list of the potholes I have hit during my life. How I wished I could have avoided them!

I have been dirt poor.

I have been abused as a child.

I have felt I was nobody from nowhere and would never amount to anything — in other words, a zero.

I have been rejected.

I have been divorced.

I have been widowed.

I have been a single parent of three children.

I have been seriously ill.

I have been extremely lonely.

I have been severely depressed.

And yet, I made it through these problems to the point where I am happy, excited about today and the future, and totally at peace. You also can make it to this same point, regardless of your problems. And you can do it by starting from where you are now.

Any obstacle, any problem will succumb to some combination of the positive actions expressed on the following pages. And I hope you will be encouraged by exposure to some new ideas and approaches. If you desire to be better — and I believe we all do — then you have already taken the first step to a happier, more fulfilling future. The next step is to construct your own personal plan of action from your own ideas and the strategies and techniques presented here and in other places. Desire...Plan...Action. These are the steps. You *can* make it better.

ENCOURAGING TRUTHS

Six of the most compelling reasons you can make your life better are what I call "encouraging truths." There are others, but for starters I'll begin with these:

1. Our engine just needs a tune-up.

2. Others will help us.

3. Success can be ours today and every day.

4. Positive actions bring positive results.

5. Life is not one game — it's a whole season.

6. All good things start small.

Our Engine Just Needs a Tune-up

Relax! The news is good. The odds are strongly in your favor that you can dramatically improve your overall performance with just a tune-up. You will not need a major overhaul. No matter what your situation or problem, very likely you will need less corrective action than you anticipate. In most people's lives, just a few small, positive changes can bring great results.

A few years ago, I read about a contest for young auto mechanics who were in the final phase of their training at various technical schools. Teams were formed of four members and an advisor from each school, and even a couple of substitutes in case an original member needed to be replaced. Then the teams were assembled, and a competition was held to determine which team could diagnose and correct various engine problems which had been preset into brand new automobiles by the competition judges. The team that could diagnose and correct the problems in the least amount of time was the winner.

The engines in the contest would barely run — if they could be started at all. The judges had for practical purposes disabled these new, powerful automobiles by afflicting them with a number of small problems, such as loose battery cables, wrong settings, and disconnected spark plugs — things like that.

The competition began and within a short time, the winner had been chosen and all the automobiles were back in perfect working order. As I read the article describing the contest, I began to see a correlation between these powerful automobile engines and something much more important.

21

Like those incredible road machines, we are designed by a Master Craftsman for long and beneficial service. But just as sophisticated mechanical or electronic equipment can be dramatically impaired or stopped by a small malfunction, so can we be completely stymied by small problems or lack of knowledge.

The exciting thing is that we — like the engines in the story — just need a tune-up and the original power and performance will return. No major overhaul is necessary. Most of the time we just need minor adjustments to get back on the road to fulfillment and happiness.

I truly believe that, almost always, the things that impair our efficiency are easily fixed and that we can repair them with God's help. Small specific changes might include a ready smile or the determination to be on time; both of these would improve our relationship with others. Organizing tasks will cut down on stress. Remember, at this time, we are talking about a tune-up, not an overhaul.

Others Will Help Us

One of the most encouraging truths is that others will help us as we strive to be better. Not everyone will help. Perhaps the ones we most wish would help us will not step forward when we need them. But some will, and their help will be sufficient for our needs. Most people get a very good feeling from helping others. But we should not expect others to rearrange their lives to help us improve ours.

The first way others will help us takes zero effort on their part, but can be very valuable to us. No verbal contact is made, and sometimes they don't even know they are assisting anyone. The idea is for us to observe talented people closely, and then use them as models for areas in which we do not feel particularly gifted or effective. When we copy the way they do things or the way they deal with situations that we do not handle well, we are being helped by them.

Try to spread your net as wide as possible, by looking for as many talented people as you can find. Then compare their way with your way, and adopt their methods if theirs are better. Find the best way to do whatever task or job you have to do. Many of the most creative ideas come from other people. You compliment them by adopting their ideas to make your own life better.

Next, ask for advice from people who have the expertise you need. You may have to catch these busy people on the run — or accept short, fast answers — but in most cases they will respond to the best of their abilities (within their time limitations) if they sense that you are sincerely seeking help.

Perhaps the best way to start is to organize your questions — even write them down. Make the questions simple, short ones that can be answered the same way. The point is to go out of the way to make it easy on the person who is providing the assistance.

If the problem is a personal one, approach the person from whom you want help in an informal environment. Make that person feel that you admire how he or she has handled a similar problem. Explain that you respect his or her experience and would appreciate using that solution. Do not create a burden by going into an endless explanation or a detailed description of your problem.

Help on business problems should be discussed in a more structured environment. Always make the person you are asking for advice feel good about his or her expertise. Explaining that your problem might improve with the use of some of those same skills, will allow him or her to help with a minimum of effort ("Your company has such an excellent reputation of conservation of resources. Could you recommend some recycling programs that I am not aware of?"). But, never, never approach a doctor or a lawyer at a dinner party and ask for a diagnosis or legal advice, no matter how good a friend that person may be!

Others will be more inclined to assist you and give better help if you do not unduly involve them in the problem. Make them part of the solution — even give them credit for the solution if you can. But try not to make your problem their problem. People like to provide help that results in the resolution of someone's problem. But they usually don't want or need all the background information that we are inclined to provide when we ask for help.

Often, when we are faced with difficult problems or situations, the tendency is to retreat from friends and people in general. It's important to fight this tendency. Remember, we all need the help of others. And other people usually want to be helpful.

Do not stop the positive in your life because of negatives. Do not quit. For instance, if you have lost your job, do not shut yourself off from friends and stop going to church.

Watch, ask, and learn.

Others will help.

Success Can Be Ours Today and Every Day

Very early in most of my speeches I tell my audiences that I am both rich and successful. Since I am often asked about that, I just go ahead and admit to it up front. I make the statement because the words *rich* and *successful* have a ring to them that appeals to me. Besides, the statement is true, and I want to make an important point.

I'm *rich* because my home in Dallas has glass window panes with screens on the outside. The home I grew up in as a child had neither glass panes nor screens on the windows. They had been knocked out years before and had never been replaced. Cardboard and cloth were all we had, so that is what we used to cover the windows. The whole house cost four hundred dollars that Mama paid off at the rate of ten dollars a month for ten years. I thought then that if I ever had a home with glass window panes and screens...then I would be rich. So today I am rich.

Why am I successful? I am *successful* because I have learned to live every day to its fullest. Most people define success in terms of things acquired, goals reached, and emotions experienced. Often a competitive factor with other people gets into their definition. I have no problem with any of those ideas. But my own definition of success is simply maintaining a continuous effort to do my best each day.

And that's what I do. I give my best effort every day. Some days I get more accomplished than on other days, but I try to give maximum effort each day.

Live every day to the fullest. Do as much good for yourself and for others as you can *each day*. That is success by any definition.

You can be a success today regardless of your yesterdays. You can be a success every day. All it takes is your best effort each day.

Positive Actions Bring Positive Results

I have deliberately stated this encouraging truth in positive terms. Too often we hear the same truth stated as "actions have consequences," and we immediately assume that the reference is to negative acts and consequences. Negative acts do result in negative consequences, but the encouraging side of this truth is that positive acts will ultimately result in positive consequences. There may be a delay in the payoff — but it is certain to occur.

♥ • ♥ • ♥ • ♥ • ♥

HEARTITUDE

You Can Be A Success Every Day

♥ • ♥ • ♥ • ♥ • ♥

Our actions decide our fate. Every positive action you take increases the probability that your goals will be reached. For sure, your life will be enriched in some manner. Your progress is slowed, however, when you delay, avoid, or decrease the number of positive actions. The best way to invest in your future is by taking as many positive actions as possible today.

Show me where people spend their money, and I will know the location of their heart. What do you think of the person on the street who smilingly drops money in the cup of a beggar? What do you think of the church tither? What do you think about people who give to the hungry, the homeless, the orphans? Whatever you think of these people, you *know* where their hearts are. When others spend money on their own pleasure exclusively, you know where *their* hearts are also. Show me the quality and quantity of a person's actions, and I will have a very good idea of that person's future prospects. Positive actions of any shape, type, or form are to be taken as often as possible. The smallest positive act can sometimes cause dramatic change for the better in your life or the life of someone else. So in reality there are no *small* positive actions — only positive actions. Take as many of them as possible. Avoid negative acts. When you do this you will take a quantum leap toward improving your life.

Life Is Not One Game — It's a Whole Season

My first encounter with the sports world came when I was a teenager and played on our high school girls' basketball team. Like most of you who played some sport in high school, I have fond memories of my days playing on the Dixie Demons. You've heard "the only game in town." Well, Dixie, Georgia, was so small that basketball was literally the only game in town, and we might have had no game at all if the rules then had called for seven players instead of six. Young people learn a lot about life from participating in sports, and it is almost always a positive experience.

In the Dallas area, we have three major professional teams, and, like many others, I have a strong interest in how well our teams are playing. Many times, an optimist would say our teams are "not doing as well as expected." The critics put it differently and in much stronger language.

But let me tell you how I rate the teams. Our three hometown teams are always first place with me, no matter what their records. When it comes to other teams, however, "Mamie's Ranking System" becomes slightly more scientific. It has three parts:

1. How cute is the coach?

2. How cute is the coach?

3. Refer to #1 and #2.

The result is that behind the Mavericks, Cowboys, and Rangers come the Los Angeles Lakers, coached by that cute Pat Riley. However, he has retired and is now a sports announcer on NBC, so I guess I'll have to watch other teams on TV more so I can see Pat Riley at work.

But let's get back to the normal sports-ranking method so I can share with you an interesting statistic I found as I looked at the records of various championship teams over recent years. Let me relate those records to life and how we can improve ourselves. A championship baseball or basketball team will end up winning about two out of every three games over an entire season. That means the best baseball team will usually *lose* over fifty games in a season while the best basketball team will taste defeat more than twenty times. The best professional football team will probably lose three of the sixteen games in the regular season. Similarly, our lives comprise a season of games, and some defeats are inevitable. We do not have to win every game to be a champion, but we must play every game to the best of our ability. We must learn from our defeats and press on to the next game.

Give your maximum effort, improve continuously, and the victories will come.

All Good Things Start Small

My church in Dallas is the Prestonwood Baptist Church, located a few blocks from my home. It is one of innumerable examples of how everything good starts small. Prestonwood Baptist Church started more than eleven years ago with a handful of dedicated people and now has over ten thousand members — a wonderful spirit of the Lord prevails there. It is my church, and I would love it regardless of size. But the point here is that it is doing great work, and it started small.

My son Brian's favorite eating place started small too, and it is now by far the biggest chain in the fast-food industry. It was started by a man whose age was fifty-something when he heard opportunity knocking. So there is a double lesson in this example: not only do good things start small, but also opportunity sometimes knocks later in life than some of us might expect. In any case, when opportunity knocked for Ray Kroc, he recognized it. After seeing the original McDonald's in California, he returned to Illinois and started his own McDonald's, the first of the chain we all know. The rest is burger history.

Electronic Data Systems, started by Ross Perot with one thousand dollars in the 1960's and sold a few years ago for several billion dollars, is still growing rapidly as a part of General Motors. The list of companies and individuals who have grown in ability and service is endless.

These major, long-term accomplishments often start under adversity and grow with difficulty. They may begin through a decision to start in a new direction with renewed vigor and determination. The result over time can be significant — valuable to society and extremely fulfilling to the individual. Remember that major corporate and individual accomplishments all begin small — and some begin later in life. So do not fret if your past is a little thin on positive results. The past is just rehearsal. Decide what you want to do, assemble your assets, change what needs to be changed, and start small. That is what the people you admire the most did when they started.

GET IT TOGETHER — HERE'S HOW:

1. Success is the desire to be better, living every day to the fullest. Today is all we have. *Carpe diem* (this Latin phrase means "seize the day").

2. We have all had setbacks and rejections, and life has been unfair to us, but we must never quit. Persevere!

3. No matter what has happened to you, I believe in you, and others do too.

4. Life is not just one game — it's a whole season. During that season we win some games, and some we lose. But it's the season's record that is important.

CHAPTER 2

SIMPLE STEPS TO "BEE" BETTER

I have always believed it is the little things that make the big difference in our lives — things like a note from a friend, a kind word, an inspiring sermon, a cold drink on a hot day, indoor plumbing. Believe me, if you grew up without it, as I did, indoor plumbing would be on your list, too. I am always grateful for every good and pleasant thing that comes my way in whatever form or size. Small and simple things are very important to me, and I hope they are to you.

Someone once said that we would get a real kick if every tenth cup of coffee tasted ten times better than the first one. I certainly agree with that thought. One cup is wonderful; but most of us gag at about cup number five. More is not always better. Bigger is certainly not always better, either.

♥ • ♥ • ♥ • ♥ • ♥

HEARTITUDE

All Good Things Start Small

♥ • ♥ • ♥ • ♥ • ♥

Simple steps to *bee** better are all I have ever known. Complex solutions cause my eyes to glaze over and my mind to scream for a more understandable answer. I am convinced that simple steps work better, no matter how complicated the problem. Little things. Small starts. Simple steps.

Is there a principle or truth here that we need to understand and use? The answer is yes. Let me state the principle this way:

MAJOR PROGRESS IN ANY AREA IS THE RESULT OF A SERIES OF SMALL POSITIVE STEPS.

*See p. 13.

Big results are always a combination of small, positive steps consistently taken over a period of time. Thus, major progress is not out of the reach of us ordinary mortals. Why? Because we can take simple steps, and keep taking them until any goal is reached.

BUILDING A BETTER YOU

Simple acts are the building blocks from which we construct the big achievements of our lives. The secret is to assemble these building blocks in a rational way to construct whatever result we desire. What are the most important and most often needed simple steps which we use to build large achievement over time?

Here are some suggestions based on choices that have worked for me:

1. Get right with God.

2. Concentrate on small improvements.

3. Start now.

4. Stop all negatives.

5. Strive for quality.

6. Stay alert for opportunity.

7. *Bee* creative.

8. Help others.

9. Never quit.

Get Right With God

Take this step and you immediately and significantly improve your chances of reaching any worthwhile goal. Many people are hindered by conflicts between their actions and their religious or moral beliefs. We are weakened by any difference between what we do and what we believe. It is vital to success to align our actions with our beliefs.

One of the most common causes of our failures is the desire to do things our own way in direct conflict with our understanding of God's way. I do not claim perfect knowledge of God's way, although I have read and studied the Bible since childhood — from title page to maps, over and over. What I do know is that we can make little or no progress in being a better person if our actions are in conflict with our understanding of God's rules for our lives.

People who steal may have money temporarily, but they can never find happiness with the money because they are thieves. It weakens us tremendously when we take any actions that are not in harmony with our religious beliefs. On the other hand, we are strengthened when we get our actions in tune with our beliefs.

My problems would have overwhelmed me if I had not been trusting in the Lord all my life. I have tried my best to live as He would have me live, and this fact has strengthened me as nothing else could have done.

Get right with God. It is the most important thing you will ever do. Retain your integrity, or regain it, if you have lost it. God's way frees you to be your best in all of your endeavors.

Concentrate on Small Improvements

You can completely change anything for the better if you will put into practice the idea of concentrating on small improvements. Think of any person, product, or organization that impresses you favorably. You are thinking of the result of many small improvements over a period of time.

Examine your life as it is and compare where you are today with the person you desire to *bee*. Now start making small improvements in all areas. Remember, I said small improvements. Do the obvious, easy ones first and establish a record of small, relatively simple positive changes: smile, speak, improve your attitude, organize your life, be on time.

Some of the modern fast-food chains have done a wonderful job of making small changes to stay abreast of the consumer market. They started out with hamburgers; then they added breakfasts and playgrounds.

Now you can get pizza and yogurt there. One small change at a time, but what a difference in the overall operation!

You may feel, as I have in the past, that there is a very big gap between where you are now and where you want to go. Just concentrate on small changes and keep making them. Many people never reach their potential because they pass up every opportunity to make small improvements. They are waiting to make "significant" improvements, not realizing that the big, positive changes in this world are the result of many small improvements.

When significant improvements do occur, you can be assured that they will be made by people who have developed the habit of making small improvements. So start now and concentrate on making small improvements.

Start Now

One of the best habits we can develop is to take action on good intentions. Start! Move! Take that first step on any worthy or necessary project. In most instances you guarantee the positive result you want by simply taking the first step.

Read the preceding sentence again. It is one of my strongest beliefs. In a high percentage of cases, you will complete the action you start. The first step gets you started and inner momentum does most of the later work. It is human nature to put off or delay starting even necessary tasks. It is also our nature to go ahead and finish a job once it is underway.

Successful people have learned to use these tendencies to their advantage. They know that if they take the first step — if they simply start — they will follow through and finish. Another common tendency is to do the job to the best of our ability once we are into a project. So the key to accomplishing any task — and doing it well — is to start.

Stop All Negatives

We are where we are today because of past decisions and actions, adjusted for circumstances beyond our control. In other words, it is what we do with what happens to us that counts. I urge you not to use less than perfect circumstances as an excuse for postponing positive changes. I am convinced that the pluses and minuses of things that are out of our control eventually balance out for all of us.

The teacher in me wants to give you my formula for positive change. It is simply this:

START POSITIVE THINGS + STOP NEGATIVE THINGS = A CHANGED AND BETTER YOU

We have already discussed how starting positive things is an integral and vital part of achieving our goals. The second important action we must take is to stop negative things. That means we need a strong campaign to eliminate negative thinking and negative actions from our lives.

I believe in the replacement theory for fighting the negatives in our lives: replace the negatives with positive thoughts and actions. Leave no room for negatives either in your mind or in your actions. By staying busy with positive acts, you will have neither time nor energy for negative actions.

You will be a changed-for-the-better person if you remember and actuate the formula for positive change.

Strive for Quality

The jet planes that whisk me from place to place never cease to amaze me, as I fly back and forth over this country in order to speak. It's reassuring to know that the United States builds the best commercial jets in the world. But while I'm interested in the quality of the planes in which I fly, my work focuses on the importance of quality in people's lives. I am convinced that we must strive for quality in all that we do.

Only by trying to be the best in all areas of our lives can we become better persons.

Do the best you can do in your work. *Bee* the best person you can *bee* in your personal life. You can buy quality in the products you use, but you cannot purchase the ingredients to make yourself a quality person. Instead, those characteristics are free to all who will put forth the effort to use them.

Quality is always highly valued in both people and products. It takes persistent effort and attention to detail. But the real secret to quality is in tiny improvements in a thousand places. Think quality. Strive for quality. Be a person of quality.

Stay Alert for Opportunity

We are all looking for something: a better job, new clients, more friends. Many of us are looking for love, or looking for purpose. We are usually looking for several things at the same time — things or people we believe can make our lives better. We need more and better opportunities to find that for which we search.

Stay alert and watch for these opportunities everywhere you go. Luck has been defined as the point where preparation and opportunity meet. Know what you are looking for, and realize that it may show up at any time, or any place.

Where is opportunity usually found? Is there a place we should look first, or do we just wander around in a constant state of watchfulness? Yes and yes.

Opportunity is most often found in the form of new people you meet. Old friends may introduce you, but the opportunity to seek new possibilities often comes through some new person in your life. Think back and you will probably find that many of the good things that have happened to you were the result of meeting new people. I know this is true in my life. You never have too many friends and quality acquaintances. So make the effort to meet new, quality people. They will provide you many additional pluses for your life — including opportunity.

Bee **Creative**

We all want to be special. I call it being different without being ridiculous. Not many of us want to be a part of a vast homogenized whole, in which everyone is the same. We want to be unique in a positive way. Being creative can set us apart, make us feel better about ourselves, and make us more attractive to other people. I want to encourage you to *bee* a more creative person in all aspects of your life. It is not as difficult to be creative as some of you are thinking.

How do we become more creative? We look for small changes that we can make in our normal, daily lives. A creative person is one who makes small changes in whatever is now considered standard or normal. Most creative people make their reputations with these small, simple changes to the established way. You can do the same. Learn to think and act creatively. Look for easier, better, and more inexpensive ways to improve all aspects of your daily life. Find a few solutions that are changes in the norm, and you are being creative.

We can help ourselves to *bee* more creative, but more than that, we can encourage those around us to develop the trait. Specifically, at school we can require students to design costumes to wear when making oral book reports, to research and carry out poster ideas, and to write original stories and poems. Some students resist these projects because they do require extra thought and brainstorming, but they usually respond positively in light of the challenge.

When our own children are working on such assignments, we parents can contribute by helping and encouraging them. At home we might require the children to make gifts and cards rather than buy them. Encourage them to write notes and draw pictures rather than just to color. In the business world, dare to be different. Brainstorm and get the job done, but do it in new and different ways. When you are thinking innovatively, this alone will motivate others to follow suit.

So keep looking and keep changing. Soon everyone will call you creative — one of the nicest compliments you can ever have.

Help Others

We help ourselves best when we help other people. Obviously, that is not an original thought, but it is certainly an accurate one. I am convinced that a strong commitment to helping other people is necessary for our own growth and happiness.

Look around and you will find that the people you admire the most, the most successful people you know, are the most helpful to others. I feel confident that we could justify helping other people simply because it helps us more than it does them. But there are better reasons for helping others.

♥ • ♥ • ♥ • ♥ • ♥

HEARTITUDE

When You Help Others You Help Yourself

♥ • ♥ • ♥ • ♥ • ♥

I help other people because it is the right thing to do, to pay back the people who have helped me; and I do it because I am happiest when I am helping others. Many people have helped me in many ways over the years. It is almost never possible to repay these people with like kindness. The only way to repay them is to pass along the help to new people, with interest. My idea of a perfect world is one where everyone helps everyone else and nobody keeps score.

Join with me and with many others in one of the first examples of the "Win-Win" philosophy:

HELP OTHERS AND THUS HELP YOURSELF.

The following ten commandments are easier said than done — after all, they are not suggestions but commandments. It's easy to say, "Don't quit." But we must carry through by thinking in terms of sticking to a purpose. Perseverance is a state of mind, a habit that we must cultivate and nurture. The determination to stick to a goal is a quality we can develop, and this quality is worth the effort. I understand. I know we all face bleak periods of frustration when things seem to get worse instead of better. But I encourage you to plod on — one inch at a time. Keep your head up. Look for the good times. I believe in you.

Never Quit

Get right with God...and never quit.

Concentrate on small improvements...and never quit.

Start now...and never quit.

Stop all negatives...and never quit.

Strive for quality...and never quit.

Stay alert for opportunity...and never quit.

Bee creative...and never quit.

Help others...and never quit.

Rest...but never quit.

Believe in yourself...and never quit.

GET IT TOGETHER — HERE'S HOW:

1. Little things can make the big difference. A smile, a thank you, a nod — all are encouragement to others. We all need to feel capable and appreciated.

2. Start with small, simple steps. Whatever your situation, start — and keep it simple. Break down every problem or job into small, bite-size pieces and begin by eliminating one problem at a time. It can be done.

3. Get your priorities right: God, family, and business.

4. Start positive things + stop negative things = a changed and better you.

5. Strive for quality in your job, your relationships, and your life. Go for quality. Think *quality* in all that you do and strive to *bee*.

CHAPTER 3

NOT GUILTY — SOME THINGS ARE NOT YOUR FAULT

Not everything that is faced can be changed, but nothing
can be changed until it is faced.

—James Baldwin

The word *guilt* actually means a feeling of remorse for wrongdoing. I will quickly add that I do hope that we always have remorse for an offense, a violation, a crime, or an act that goes against what we know is morally right. However, much of our guilt is not actually real; it is false. Many things happen to us that we cannot control, and we feel guilty about them. But we shouldn't.

TAKE <u>U</u> OUT OF GUILT

When the *u* is taken out of *guilt,* we have the word *gilt,* which means a thin layer of gold. According to the dictionary, gold means precious, valuable, and free from the liability of rusting. When I relate this to our lives, it is easy for me to understand that many people suffer from feelings of hopelessness, uselessness, and depression because they have "rusted" with guilt in their thoughts and actions. This "rusted" feeling of anxiety, fear, pain, and uneasiness keeps us from using our talents and abilities. Mark Twain said, "Conscience fills more than all the rest of a person's insides."

There are many unfair things that happen to all of us from time to time. Bad things do happen, even to good people. We must realize that

♥•♥•♥•♥•♥

HEARTITUDE

The Most

Beautiful

Gift of All Is

Forgiveness

♥•♥•♥•♥•♥

these things are often not our fault. The only fault that is ours is not handling what happens to us. We must learn to face, to trace, and to erase these problems. The Bible states in Philippians 3:13 that we must move on, "forgetting those things which are behind [past]," and yet we fret and remember them vividly. We allow these thoughts of guilt to control us and pull us down emotionally and physically.

Medical doctors agree that this kind of unrest, when left inside us, will cause medical and psychological problems. When we suppress guilt and let it seethe, it will affect our total being — outside as well as inside. Often it will be evident in the way we walk, talk, and interact with others. Other times we can put up a false front so that others will never know how we really feel about ourselves. We do this because we do not want others to know and judge us too harshly.

MAKING A MISTAKE IS NO REASON TO
LIVE AS A MISTAKE

Many of you have read my first book, *I Can. You Can Too!* In it I related the story of how I married the first time at the age of twenty-eight, truly believing that it was the right thing to do. But after five months of marriage I came home one day to find a note from my husband on my front door saying, "I don't want any part of you, your family, the home, or church — I'm leaving." Even now, more than two decades later, I find it difficult to express the feelings of helplessness and hopelessness I felt as I read that note. In my first book, I described those feelings this way:

> Unless you have had the wind knocked out of you by a kick in the stomach, you cannot imagine how I felt at that moment. All I had experienced when I was an abused child — the nausea, the fear, the "dirty" feelings — swept over me like an ice cold winter wind. The inferior feelings I had felt when I started to college, the mocking of grade school children, the embarrassment of hand-me-down clothes — everything negative that I

had ever experienced flashed through my mind in one sickening instant.

From this divorce I learned that you cannot make people love you. My experience has been that if a person wants a divorce badly enough, you cannot make him or her change. I begged, pleaded, cried, prayed, and went through counseling. I did everything I could do to make it work, but to no avail. For a year after the divorce, I prayed that my ex-husband would change his mind and come back — but that just did not happen. I literally gave up on life. I quit my job and returned to Dixie, Georgia, to die — depressed, sad, lonely, dejected, and unable to forgive myself because of what had happened. I went home to sit on my mama's front porch and die.

The psychologists tell us that depression is anger turned inward. My anger smoldered, which was the reason for my year-long depression. In those years after the divorce, my guilt screamed out again and again inside my head, *What could I have done differently to have made it work!* You see, I was divorced, and I did not even believe in divorce. I had been reared in a society that condemned it. But the reality was that I was divorced and could do nothing about it. I had to accept this failure and "go on down the road."

Although the guilt about my failed first marriage continued to haunt me, I did find great happiness as I moved on. I married again, reared a family with my new husband, and experienced joy — if not total peace of mind — until my second husband died in 1981.

HEALING IS POSSIBLE

❧

On a cool fall night in October, 1987, I was attending a birthday party for a friend of mine. I was hesitant about accepting the invitation because I knew I would be going alone, I would not know many of the guests, and frankly I feared being a wallflower. Also, I was very careful not to accept nighttime social events, because my traveling already took me away from my children more than I liked.

Nevertheless, I went to the party and tried to fit in. I began introducing myself and making general conversation. As I stood chatting with one of the guests, I noticed a man in a beautiful leather jacket moving about the room. I never looked him in the face, but I did notice his jacket. Later, I heard someone say, "Aren't you going to speak to me?" I turned around to find myself face to face with my first husband for the first time since our divorce twenty years before. I had not seen him, nor did I know that he lived several blocks away from us in Dallas. To say we were both surprised, shocked, and embarrassed would be an understatement. We stood there looking at each other as if we had each seen a ghost. I recovered first, realizing this was my chance to ask him the question I had asked myself so often in the past twenty years. "Was it my fault? Could I have done anything differently to have kept us both from the heartache?"

His reply was what I had desperately needed to hear: "Mamie, it was not your fault. There was nothing you could have done to have made it work; it was my fault, not yours."

You see, I had to hear those words from the one who had caused the grief. I was reminded again how many people endure pain that is beyond their control. I also realized that on October 13, 1987, I began the real healing process. The weight had been lifted and I felt so free. Probably no one noticed that I looked or acted differently, but I felt the vise had been loosened. I had finally forgiven myself, and in turn I could forgive him. Facing my former husband had freed me from my guilt of a broken marriage and allowed me to freely forgive.

IT'S OKAY TO GET HELP

There are times in the lives of all of us when we need professional counseling. We should not feel embarrassed because we need someone to help us through the tough times. But we should seek out those professionals who are most able to assist us. When my teeth hurt, I immediately call my dentist. I don't tell my foot doctor that my teeth hurt — I tell my dentist. I once heard someone say, "Don't ever tell any problem to anyone who cannot help you solve it." Whatever our problems are, there are people all around us who are trained to help us solve them.

In 1986, I felt the need to visit the Pritikin Longevity Center in California. I had been having chest pains ever since my second husband died in 1981. I thought it was just because of the strain of raising three small children, along with my speaking and traveling schedule. I was checked each year by my general practitioner, and I was always told my heart was fine. However, sometimes the pain in my chest would be so intense that I could hardly breathe.

When I finished the extensive medical examination at Pritikin, I was told that I had no heart or medical problems. But why had I felt so depressed? And why did I have no energy, no motivation? This did not mean I did not function. I continued to speak, travel, and be Mama, but I never felt good anymore and I cried a lot — only in private, of course. After all, I was a motivational speaker and my mission was to make people feel good, loved, and appreciated. At that time I was much better at making others feel better about themselves than I was at making myself feel good.

DEPRESSION CAN KILL YOU
☙

When the head physician at Pritikin gave me a clean bill of health, I should have been relieved, but I wasn't. I was still hurting very much; I had the feeling that a rubber band was squeezing me to death. At times I could hardly breathe because, I hurt so badly. When I explained how I felt, he told me something I did not want to hear: "Mrs. McCullough, you must see our counselor."

Me? I thought. *Why me? Surely he must be wrong. I don't need a counselor. After all, I am a Christian, and Christians don't need this type of therapy.*

The physician explained that to get well and feel good again, I had to seek counseling. I was crushed, but I did finally decide to take his advice. During the first three days I only cried. Eventually, the counselor said, "Mamie, you are depressed because you have never given up your husband." I was shocked. Surely I had — I had been with him when he died. Yes, I had given him up. Then she asked that I write him a good-bye letter. Although I felt that was certainly not necessary, I did it. It was an eight-page letter, and feelings of anger poured out of me as I wrote. I discovered that I had suppressed anger, because I was left with three small children, with total responsibility for the house, and with all the threatening problems of being a single parent.

When I went for my next visit, the counselor asked that I read the letter to her. Reluctantly, I read it aloud, and as I did, I felt relief and a peace that I had not experienced in a long, long time. She explained how I had felt it necessary to carry on after my husband's death and had not processed my feelings of grief.

CLIMBING THE STEPS OF GRIEF

You see, when my husband died unexpectedly at the young age of forty-six, I was left with three children ages five, six, and eight. I returned to my speaking schedule only eight days after the funeral. No one ever placed this responsibility on me — I did it to myself. People would have understood if I had canceled a speech, but I felt it was my job and I had to do it. However, it was to my detriment that I tried to return to "normal" so quickly.

The process of grief has certain stages or steps that can be expected, but not predicted as to how and when they will happen. It is not a scheduled flight that takes off from "grief" and lands in "peace" within a set time frame. Nor is there a prearranged order to the steps of grief. Many grieving people follow the steps in a similar sequence, while others bounce from one to the other in a totally different order. No matter how we climb them, though, there is no way we can skip any of these steps:

1. *Denial.* Almost always the first response, this feeling is one of shock and disbelief: *This cannot be happening to me!*

2. *Anger turned outward.* We want to cry, talk, and cry some more; then scream, or even fight. We are angry.

3. *Anger turned inward.* This occurs when we have talked a lot, cried a lot, and then quit showing our grief to others.

4. *Genuine grief.* This is the flooding of emotions and grief on special occasions or when we encounter certain people and places.

5. *Resolution.* This acceptance of loss is accompanied by reaffirmation of the reality of life.

Grief is best defined as "any significant loss." We have to realize that we are all human and that the losses which cause us emotional upset may range from the loss of a friend to a "lost" marriage, from the loss of a job to the loss of a child. There are many physical and emotional characteristics that accompany the grief we feel when we suffer a loss. By being aware of these characteristics, we can better understand the process of grief. Then we can work through the process so our grief does not become debilitating, and we can get on with life.

Because I did not properly grieve after my divorce or after the death of my husband, I suffered depression for several years. This possibly could have been prevented had I turned to counselors who could have helped me understand grief.

When grief is not processed, it is bottled up inside us, like steam in a boiling pot waiting for the lid to be loosened. When the doctor at Pritikin explained how I could begin to release my old guilt and grief, it was as if I had also been released from the hurt, the heartache, the pressure, and the strain. He outlined a year-long program for me, which I followed closely. And you know something? It worked! What they really wanted to help me do — just as I want to help you do — is to *let go!*

WHEN WE LET GO, WE LET GOD

Letting go is to fear less — and love more.

Letting go is not to regret the past — but to grow and live.

Letting go is not to deny — but to accept.

Letting go is not to cut ourselves off from others.

Letting go is not to try to change or blame others — but to make the most of ourselves.

Letting go is to quit blaming ourselves for what we cannot change — but to continue to place our lives in the Lord Who made us.

Letting go means letting God.

When you feel you need help in letting go of the grief and anger in your life, I encourage you to seek the kind of help which will enable you to grow and process the hurts. I am often asked how to seek a counselor. In case you are asking the same question, here are some suggestions:

1. Solicit referrals from your doctor, pastor, and friends.

2. Decide the type of help you need or want, that is, family therapy, marital counseling, issue-oriented individual counseling (recovery from alcoholism, sexual abuse, etc.).

3. Decide whether you want a male or female counselor.

4. Decide if you want to pay more to get a licensed and experienced counselor, or if you would rather save expenses and see an intern.

5. Look for a counselor with values and beliefs similar to your own.

6. Call and interview potential counselors. They should be willing to talk with you over the phone and answer your questions.

When you are in the valley of grief, do not make a major change in your life. Many people have told me of having had feelings of depression that led to their quitting their jobs or dissolving their marriages, only to regret this action in a few weeks or months. When you are hurting so badly, I would encourage you to remain as constant as possible with things you can influence — your family, your church attendance, and your job. When problems arise in one area of our lives, we must try to keep the other areas from being affected.

TURN LOOSE — *BEE* **FREE**

Do you know how the natives used to catch monkeys in the islands? They would cut a hole in the top of a coconut, hollow it out, and fill it with sweet beans. The monkey would reach in the coconut and grab the beans, making a fist as he did so. With his hand rolled into a fist, he could not pull his hand back through the opening in the coconut because he wouldn't let go of the beans. So in the morning, the monkey was still trapped there, and the natives only had to come by and pick him up.

Sometimes we find ourselves trapped simply because we won't let go of all our past grudges, resentments, bitterness, guilt over past sins, and unrealistic expectations of ourselves and others. As my mother used to tell us, your hands cannot be filled with God's blessings of peace, joy, happiness, contentment, or fulfillment when your fists are not free to receive these gifts. This story about the monkey illustrates well my present feeling of joy.

With the counselor's help, I was willing to empty my hands and heart of past guilt placed on me by society, and to forgive myself for the first time in many years. Oh, what a relief that was! I still could not change what had happened to me, but I finally had learned to accept what had happened and get on with life.

What is it in your life that has you trapped because you won't let go of it?

The scars of my divorce will always be there, but I don't bleed anymore. Even though many people had tried to tell me the divorce was not my fault, I could not hear what they were saying. But when my former husband admitted responsibility, I truly began a new life of self-forgiveness, free of guilt.

FEELING HURT IS BETTER
THAN FEELING NOTHING

We often look at others whom we feel we know so well and judge them only from what we see on the outside. Evelyn, one of my older sisters, has taught me a lot about this. She is a jolly person, well liked by her peers; she smiles and is a very contented lady. However, if you knew her background, you would wonder why she ever had anything to smile about.

She got married right out of high school to a local young man. He was good-looking and his family owned one of the largest land acreages in the county. Evelyn and her husband had five beautiful children. Then, after about ten years of marriage, he began running around on her. He was an alcoholic, as well as a womanizer; he never attended church or family gatherings. Evelyn never talked about it or admitted it. For twenty-five years, she endured his abusive treatment. Then on the advice of many people who feared for her life, she left her husband and came to Texas where my sister Martha Ann and her husband, Ray Blundell, helped her get her nurse's training.

Evelyn eventually got a divorce. Like me, she did not believe in divorce, but she knew her husband was living with another woman, and felt she had no choice.

About five years ago, she was on the way to Dallas to visit me when I received a call saying that her ex-husband had died from cancer. Evelyn did not yet know. When she arrived, I was the one to break the news to her. To my surprise, she cried and cried. When she regained her composure much later that night, I asked her what her feelings were, and she replied, "Mamie, I have no hope now; he is dead. I thought someday he would come back and tell me that I was the only one he had ever loved."

What an awakening that was for me! We can never look at a wound and tell how deep the hurt is.

Several years later, Evelyn met a rancher in South Texas who treated her with love and respect, and they have been happily married for over a year now. They are both in their golden years and count each day as a blessing. See — you can make it! You never know when the "it" in your life will change — hopefully for the better.

The freedom that comes from facing a situation and processing it is indescribable. Then peace, joy, contentment, and a feeling of fulfillment are abundant. These gifts were not nearly so evident in my life until I faced my guilt. My sister felt that hanging on to the hurt was better than nothing. Then she discovered that God gave her new direction, new purpose, and a new life when she let go.

Talking about divorce is not pleasant, but it is a fact of life in today's society. I am discussing it for you readers who have been hurt, who have felt guilty and undeserving of happiness. All of us are touched in some way by divorce. It is not a respecter of age, race, geographical boundaries, or size of family. And, according to projections, the divorce rate will continue to rise.

YOU ARE "THUMBBODY"

One of my mentors and role models, the late Mary Crowley, wrote a little book entitled *You Are Somebody*. She said that God does not make a nobody. He is entirely too busy to waste His time making a nobody. However, many of us do not believe what the Bible actually says about that subject.

When my children were small and I was so interested in their having good self-images and feeling good about using their talents and abilities, I came up with the idea that each of us is a "thumbbody." With all the people in the world, there are no two thumbprints alike. Billions of people have walked on this earth, and each has had his own unique set of thumbprints. When I give the "thumbs-up" sign, I am saying to others, "You are thumbbody." No one else can use your unique talents or abilities — you are the only one in existence who can do that.

I received a beautiful note from Trish Lilly, who sang at a Fellowship of Christian Athletes banquet where I spoke. Her note said: "The first time I remember seeing you was when I sang — you gave me the thumbs-up sign, and it was a sign of encouragement to me." She thanked me for helping her to feel loved and appreciated.

GET RID OF THE BASEBALL BAT
☙

No wonder so many people are "beaten up" with life. I'm not talking about the abuse from others — I'm talking about people abusing themselves. They go through life hitting themselves over the head with thoughts like: *I'm too fat or I'm too short or I'm not bright or I'm dumb or I'm not pretty or handsome. I'm, I'm, I'm....*Or they worry: *I should go back to school, I should apply myself, I should be more friendly* — on and on and on.

Each time they say "I'm," "I shouldn't," or "I should," they are mentally hitting themselves over the head with a baseball bat. No wonder people feel the weight of the world; their problems seem to be magnified. Get rid of the bat! It causes us to feel guilty. We are so busy beating ourselves up that we have no time to build ourselves up. We must direct our energy upward, not downward. Remember: *God turns hurt hearts into healed helpers.*

Just as we are all created differently, our abilities to deal with stress are different. We're like the various trees in the forest: some of us can withstand difficult, strong storms of stress and abuse better than others. I like the example of the palm tree, which can endure both storms and drought, because it is said to have a living heart and is not affected on the exterior by the hardships of the weather.

Similarly, by maintaining a renewed heart daily, we are given help to stand strong. The leaves of the palm tree are long and slender, and the winds cannot destroy them. Hurricane winds often break ordinary trees, but the flexible palm bows to the ground and springs back when the storm has passed. Palm roots are thick and strong and go deep into the ground. And, as a palm tree ages, its fruit grows sweeter.

So it is with our lives — we are all scarred, beaten down, tested, and treated unfairly at times. Still, we can survive — and grow. The psalmist wrote, "The righteous shall flourish like the palm tree" (Psalm 92:12). We need to learn to flourish even when everything around us is unfruitful. To do this, we have to be rooted in our commitment to excellence and integrity. *Only what we have wrought into our character during life can we take with us.*

We need to make a personal commitment to be builders of others. This is how we build, grow, and learn to *bee* all that God wants us to be. As Mary Crowley so aptly put it, "If it is to be, it is up to me."

ERASE OLD TAPES

My beautiful friend Nell visited me last year at a very difficult time in her life. She was in top management with a very large company, lived in a beautiful new home, had a lovely, loving family; however, her depression was so bad that she was talking about wishing to end it all. To look at her, one would most certainly think, *She has the world by the tail.* However, she was hurting so badly that she could barely talk at times. During her visit, my family and I encouraged her and loved her. We prayed with her and did all we knew to do to make her feel special, loved, and capable. Toward the end of her visit, she finally revealed that one of the reasons she felt so bad about herself was an old tape that kept running through her mind on a daily basis.

When she was about fourteen years old, her father had made a statement about her that she could not process. She admitted that at fourteen she was a gangly size and had very bad skin. But she was not prepared to hear her father tell her mother one day, "Get Nell out of my sight with that ugly face." Throughout her life, Nell had been unable to accept her true image of beauty, charm, poise, and love because of that one statement — that tape that continued to play on and on in her mind. Complicating this was a certain amount of guilt Nell felt because she had not been able to erase this tape. I encouraged her to write her father a letter. Even though she did not send it to him, she read it to a friend and got many hurtful feelings out of her system. It was relief from an old hurt.

Please, please, one way or another, get rid of those old detrimental tapes.

Besides writing a letter, what else can we do to help ourselves? There are several things: quit replaying these tapes; turn them off. Consciously replace hurtful memories by pushing them aside with pleasant thoughts. We usually do not have positive and negative thoughts at the same time. Make a real effort to forgive the one who caused the hurt. Fill your life with purpose; pray; enlarge your circle of friends; and stay busy. People who fill their lives with worthwhile endeavors rarely have time to relive old hurts.

The sum and substance of my discussion about unrealistic guilt is that it is usually a self-inflicted emotion, often about a situation over which we have no control. But we can escape from the guilt trap by facing the problem, looking it in the eye and staring it down. Then we must trace the experience—get to its roots and analyze it. And next we must erase that old tape, whatever it is that caused the hurt and guilt. **Face, trace, and erase**. Then turn it loose and get on with your life.

PROCESS GUILT

As we noted at the beginning of this chapter, we have a tremendous amount of guilt in our lives, some of it true guilt, and some of it false. We need to understand that some things in life are just a "done deal," that our only choice is to accept them as such, and then get busy with our lives today. We can never live yesterday again, so we should not waste time trying to. We can no more live yesterday than we can unring a bell.

Women in recent decades have had even more guilt placed on them because of the social climate in the workforce. Many times I have stated that I have always worked outside the home because of necessity. From the time I was eight years old I have been working and helping to buy clothes and food, not only for myself but for other members of my family as well. It has not been all good. But neither has it been all bad. In many ways it has been a blessing, because I have been able to enjoy jobs that were a challenge, and I have had some beneficial experiences because of my work.

As I travel across the country speaking to schools, businesses, and churches, I find that one of the most-asked questions is, "How can you be away from your children and not feel guilty?" The answer is simple: I will not allow others to dictate my attitude. Whether it was growing up in Dixie, Georgia, or being left widowed with three small children, I have never felt I had a choice in working, and I feel that I am doing what the Lord wants me to do by speaking and writing.

If Mamie McCullough is to reach out and encourage others and help them to grow, she has no choice but to travel. Taking this into consideration, I made the decision not to allow others to place guilt and blame on me for doing this work. It is a decision which I have to deal with even now. I believe people do not realize what they are saying or asking when they bring up the question, "Why are you working outside the home?" Be real. This is the '90s, folks, and it has become a way of life — sometimes by choice, but most of the time by necessity. This is a new era, and women will be an even greater influence in the workforce.

I have never had the opportunity to "stay at home." I wish I could have experienced that, but it did not happen. If it is your choice to work and help with the family's financial responsibilities, do it and don't allow others to dictate how you feel about it. It is ironic that some of my friends who do "stay at home" have guilt placed on themselves for not working outside the home.

Someone sent me a copy of the "Working Mother's Creed" from a wall plaque in a local craft shop. I thought perhaps you would enjoy it:

Now I sit me down to work

And pray that I don't go berserk,

But manage somehow to succeed,

Do the job with skill and speed,

Keep disaster well at bay,

Make it through another day;

Then head home to errands galore,

Car pool, marketing, and even more,

Dinner to fix and dishes to do,

Cleaning, dusting, laundry too . . .

All for the love of a family.

But remember the magic words:

I CAN

Whether we work in the home full time or make the choice to work outside the home, women have a tremendous role to fill; and we all have more than we can get done. I would like to challenge you — at whatever stage you are — to evaluate your situation and have some time to enjoy life. Take a rest. Take a nap. Smell the roses. God knows our every need, and as indicated in chapter 31 of the Book of Proverbs, it's not an easy job, but with God's help, we can do it!

♥ • ♥ • ♥ • ♥ • ♥

HEARTITUDE

Take Time

To Smell

the Roses

♥ • ♥ • ♥ • ♥ • ♥

DOING IT ALL IS NOT NECESSARY

Through the years, I have been told that I am a perfectionist. Those of you who know a perfectionist realize the problems with wanting to have things neat and straight and in their places. Also, I find myself expecting others to work as hard as I work. This has been an unconscious attitude, and I've had to lighten up on my expectations of others, who could begin to feel a great deal of guilt when "perfection" might often be an impossibility.

The "perfectionist syndrome" may even be called the "supermom syndrome." We feel we must get everything done and done right, and in the process we may make our co-workers and the members of our family feel uncomfortable. To escape this situation, we need to decide our priorities. (For a more in-depth discussion of priorities, see Chapter 5, "Dust Is a Protective Coating for Furniture.") We also need to know what our personal limits are. When we stretch our limits, we place on ourselves a tremendous amount of stress, which causes guilt, which causes a poor self-image, which causes negative attitudes, which causes us to lose friends, and on and on and on. It is not worth it to live under the fallacy that we must "do it all." *All* is not even necessary. In fact, it's harmful! Take it from me — I have made enough of those errors to be classified as an expert.

How I would love to do all the cooking at my home, because cooking is therapy for me. But I cannot travel, write, speak, and do all the washing, ironing, cleaning, canning, and cooking that my mama did in the '30's. Times and conditions have changed. Life is hard, but it can be fun and rewarding, and you can live at peace. Do what you can, accept what you cannot do, and don't feel guilty about either. Take the "u" out of guilt. Yes, even in this day and time, it can be done!

GET IT TOGETHER — HERE'S HOW:

1. Take the "*u*" out of *guilt*. Some things are not your fault. Understand and process the fact that there will be things said to you, things done to you, and things around you which you cannot control.

2. Learn to heal. Process things that happen to you. When you are hurt, do not stop there. Acknowledge the anger — even hate. Then get help and healing begins. It is a cycle — the hurt will leave scars, but the pain lessens.

3. Remember, it's okay to receive help. We often feel intimidated because we cannot handle or adjust to every situation that comes our way. That is why we have medical doctors, dentists, spiritual doctors, counselors, and people who can help us process life's trials.

4. Get rid of all grudges. When we hold grudges — feelings of ill will and resentment — we become indifferent, calloused, and negative. It is like trying to keep pent-up steam from exploding. Instead, concentrate on turning bitterness to betterness.

5. Quit beating up on yourself. Understand that you are special and only you can use your ability. Lighten up — don't be so hard on yourself. We all fail at times. Do not look back — look forward.

CHAPTER 4

MAKING EACH DAY A BLUE RIBBON DAY

YOU'RE SPECIAL — in all the world there is nobody like you. Since the beginning of time, there has never been another person like you. Nobody has your smile. Nobody has your eyes, your nose, your hair, your hands, your voice. You're special.

No one sees things just as you do. In all of time there has been no one who laughs like you, no one who cries like you. And what makes you laugh and cry will never provoke identical laughter and tears from anybody else, ever.

You are the only one in God's creation with your set of natural abilities. There will always be somebody who is better at one of the things you're good at, but no one in the universe can reach the quality of your combination of talents, ideas, natural abilities, and spiritual abilities. Like a room full of musical instruments, some may excel alone but none can match the symphony sound of the Body of Christ when all are played together because God set the members, every one of them, in the Body as it hath pleased Him.

♥ • ♥ • ♥ • ♥ • ♥

HEARTITUDE

You Deserve a Blue Ribbon Today (If You Do Your Best)

♥ • ♥ • ♥ • ♥ • ♥

Through all of eternity no one will ever look, talk, walk, think, or do exactly like you. You're special.

You're rare. And, as in all rarity, there is great value. Because of your great rare value you need not attempt to imitate others. You should accept — yes, celebrate — your differences. You're special. Continue to realize it's not an accident that you're special. Continue to see that God created you special for a very special purpose. He called you out and ordained you to a calling that no one else can do as well as you. Out of all the billions of applicants, only one is qualified, only one has the best combination of what it takes. Just as surely as every snowflake that falls has a perfect design and no two designs are the same, so it is within the Body of Christ also. No two believers are the same; and without each member, the Body would be lacking and God's plan would be incomplete. Ask the Father to teach you His divine plan for your life and that it may stand forth revealed to you as it should, unfolding in perfect sequence and perfect order in such a way as to bring the greatest glory to His name.

—Author Unknown

As I wrote in the Introduction to this book, I began telling my story ten years ago. During that time I have often wondered how many people grew up as I did, with problems of poor self-image, and unaware, as this little essay from a wall plaque proclaims, of how special each of us really is. From the letters I get, it is quite obvious that many did. Even as adults, we all struggle with self-image in some degree.

Self-image is a system of pictures and feelings we construct about ourselves. It is the heart of our personalities: "For as [a man] thinketh in his heart, so is he" (Prov. 23:7). Many of the experts with whom I am associated believe that poor self-image is the real root of most people's personal problems. We just do not believe that we deserve anything better than the problems we face. But we do deserve better! We must determine that every day we live is special — that we deserve a blue ribbon every day. We give ourselves mental ribbons, but sometimes our efforts only win us a red or a white ribbon. It takes our best effort and the right attitude to win those blue ribbons.

EVERYONE HAS A TOUGH TIME SOMETIME

Eight o'clock on a hot summer morning was the only time I could visit Dianne. A close friend knew that this young woman was having some serious problems and had asked me to spend a few minutes with Dianne. Although I was spending eight to sixteen hours a day writing, I felt compelled to meet her at a local coffee shop. I had never met Dianne and did not know her background. We began our conversation with the usual exchange of mutual friends. From the moment I saw her, I thought, *She couldn't have a problem. Be real.* She was a tall, thin, beautiful brunette, very well groomed and very bright. However, as she began telling me about her problem, it was again quite evident to me that *everyone* has a tough time in some area of life.

Dianne had been reared in a strict Catholic family. She was one of three children. Her father was a lawyer, and they were very well-to-do. Dianne did well in high school and college, including such sports as tennis and swimming. She was twenty-eight and had never been married, but now she had found "Mr. Right." Her problem was her self-image. "Why can't I be beautiful? Why can't I be like other girls who have flawless skin?" she asked.

I was amazed at this intelligent young lady with gorgeous hair and beautiful features who was telling me she had terrible skin and a few wrinkles. She was worried that in ten years she was going to be an old woman with blemishes. She had always been told how talented and beautiful she was. She could not remember ever being told anything negative or being put down. Yet, here she sat crying because of her looks. What I saw was indeed a beautiful young lady who was her own worst enemy.

The great comic-strip philosopher Pogo once said: "We has met the enemy, and it is us." How true! We never see ourselves as others see us, and we often do become our own worst critic. Dianne admitted that she had adopted our society's attitude that the most important part of our existence is how we look on the outside, rather than how pure, good, and deserving we are inside. She visualized that perhaps as she got older, her husband would be disappointed in her looks and would leave her.

The story of Dianne is an ongoing one. After months of counseling with her, I was able to convince her that physical beauty did not deserve the importance she had placed on it. Recognizing the problem is half the battle; she began to focus on inner values. Dianne's "Mr. Right" did many of the right things also. He became more sensitive to her needs, more patient and understanding. (We *can* help each other.) The couple postponed the wedding day, but they are gradually working their way toward a happy ending. I am sorry I cannot assure you readers of this result, but the outlook is more promising than it was when Dianne and I first met.

We have been told by "modern culture" that we must be young, thin, and rich to be successful and "in." This is not true. I say it is time that we turn back to the basic values of what is really important. It is time that we focus on what we are on the inside, rather than what we look like on the outside. Now I'll admit that my hair is shaded (it faded, so I shaded it). But I'm at an "interesting" age, and my wealth lies in my family, friends, and Christian beliefs. For this, I consider myself successful — and fabulously rich.

Living up to our potential means accepting our flaws and short-comings (we all have them) and making the most of our lives. Every day is important and *today* is the *only* day we can use. To paraphrase a motto of the 1970's, "Today is the first day of the rest of our lives."

TO COPE AND TO HOPE

My meeting with Dianne made me realize how sad and angry I am at what we have allowed the values of our society to become. But we can change those values. Yes, I can — and you can too. We can make a difference. We can focus our hearts on the things of real value and help others to cope and to hope. We all must be reminded from time to time to look at what we have and not so much at what we don't have. And when we look at what we have and at what we've accomplished, we should realize that we deserve a blue ribbon — today.

After writing from 6:30 a.m. until 9 p.m. yesterday, I decided that I needed a break. I went into our den where one of my children, Jennifer, was watching "20/20" on television. The segment I saw was about teenagers who were having plastic surgery to change a chin, a nose, a breast.

Isn't it interesting how these young people cannot even wait until they are grown to change? What is this telling us about our society? I'm afraid it is saying, "Hey, if it can be fixed, you will be beautiful inside and outside," which is not necessarily true. And what are the psychological aspects? When one's appearance is fixed, does it mean that everything else is fixed? No. Life is one "fix" after another. Some things, like the aging process, cannot be stopped — slowed, perhaps, but not stopped. We will never be perfect on this earth — that's what heaven is for.

I certainly do not think that "having things fixed" is wrong. (As you may know, I had my nose fixed at the age of twenty-six.) But there is a time and a place and a level of maturity that is important for this kind of decision-making. We must teach our children that the true values of life are character traits, such as honesty, integrity, and loyalty.

MAMIE MCCULLOUGH AND ASSOCIATES

In October, 1989, I organized my company, Mamie McCullough and Associates. I laughingly say my first associates were my three teenagers, Patti, Brian, and Jennifer. They have been a real asset in helping with mailing, telephoning, and running all sorts of errands for my new company.

One evening recently I asked the children to help get out our newsletter, *The Encourager*. I requested a few hours of their time on a Friday night. They were not exuberant about having to stuff envelopes, while their friends were at the ball game or the movies. They were pleasant about it, though, and all three gathered in the glassed-in porch next to the kitchen to help. My good friends Jan Fry and Herschel Wells were helping at the kitchen table.

At first, the children thought it was rather fun; then, after about two hours it got rather quiet, and I heard Jennifer say, "Are we getting paid for this?" Brian quickly retorted, "Knowing Mama, she'll say this is one of those 'making memory' times." I could not help but snicker, remembering some of those planned "making memory" activities which I hold dear and often refer to in my speeches.

You Need To Be First Place at Home

One of those "making memory" times occurred on a Saturday several years ago, when I decided to judge the mud pies which my children had made in our backyard. They were the most beautiful mud pies I had ever seen — some had hybrid irises from the neighbor's yard, roses from another yard, and, yes, some flowering weeds from the creek behind our house. When I went out to judge the pies, there stood eight children — my own plus neighborhood friends — standing proudly behind their pies displayed on our backyard picnic table. When I had boasted to the children that I would be the judge, I had no idea what I would give as prizes. I had to use my creativity, so I cut off three blue ribbons from the children's ribbon box for first prize, three reds for second prize, and two whites for third prize. I thought each child should receive a prize for effort.

To the first three children — Patti, Jennifer, and Brian — I gave each of the blue ribbons. I did it before I thought about being their mother, so I was surprised when the other five children got mad and went home. I really did it before I thought — and I was not about to take it back. Anyway, if the other kids wanted to get first place, perhaps they should have gotten *their* mamas to judge. You see, what I want my children to remember about that day is, "If I cannot be first place (blue ribbon) in my yard, then where *can* I feel first, loved, and important?" The symbol of a blue ribbon represents unconditional love — not *like* — but love. We never do everything as others would *like,* but love can change hearts, homes, and attitudes. The Scriptures command that we love each other.

I believe we each need to take an inventory at the end of every day and decide what kind of ribbon we deserve for our efforts. If we do our very best — first-prize blue ribbon. If we almost do our best — second-prize red ribbon. If we try — third-prize white ribbon. The only time a ribbon is not appropriate is when we quit without trying at all.

Each night we need to feel we have placed in the top three. This is the feeling that, as my good friend John West says, "keeps us keepin' on." We may not always be first or second, but we can be third simply by giving continuous effort. And our best effort always deserves a blue ribbon.

One reminder: first place does not mean you are bigger or better than others. It simply means that when we use all our talents and resources on a daily basis, then we truly do deserve first-place feelings.

Turn Up Your Deserve Level

Have you measured how much you deserve out of life? When our self-images are low, our "deserve levels" are usually low. It is my desire that you feel good about yourself, and some of us have to work harder at this than others. But do not forget that you and only you can use your talents and abilities, and when you use them as best as you can on a daily basis, then you have a high deserve level. You will then feel good inside, be able to cope better, take stress better, and be a better friend to family and others.

A poor self-image carries serious effects, so we are not dealing with a trivial matter. People react or respond differently to any given situation, but typical symptoms of a poor self-image might include depression, anger, hopelessness, unwillingness to try anything new, eating disorders, alcoholism, drug abuse, feelings of rejection and isolation, physical aches and pains, failure, and, in some extreme cases, suicide. All of these manifestations are difficult to cope with. But it is said that if you recognize a problem, the battle is half won. When you understand why you have that problem, you are three-fourths of the way to solving the problem.

So let's face it: some of us have poor self-images. (We're halfway there!) Now, let's try to understand the reasons for our poor self-images. There could be a different reason for every person in the universe. Here are some common examples:

1. *Childhood memories:* "You are not good." "You are ugly." "Can't you do anything right?" "You will never amount to anything."

2. *Child abuse:* verbal, emotional, sexual, physical. Eighty-eight percent of the time, victims are abused by members of their own families. Seventy percent of the drug addicts and 75 percent of imprisoned convicts were victims of abuse. (My next book, *I Wish I Had Someone to Take Up for Me*, will deal with abuse.) Any one type of abuse will cause many problems within an individual.

3. *Put-downs:* We live in a "put-down" age. Some modern comics have built a career on this method. But these hurtful remarks aren't funny when they become personal attacks. When someone we admire puts us down, it is demoralizing.

4. *Lack of skills or education:* dropping out of school at an early age. I've never heard anyone say he or she regretted obtaining an education. However, I've heard many people express their disappointment in their *lack* of education.

5. *Disabilities:* physical and mental. Physical or learning disabilities are not something we have control over; they may be caused by heredity or by accidents which cause handicaps. We can only accept these handicaps and make the most of situations. We must remember to compare our abilities — both physical and mental — only to ourselves, not to others.

6. *Rejection:* the number one hurt to overcome. Psychologists tell us that the rejection of a child by a parent is the toughest to process. Suggestions for overcoming rejection are offered in chapter nine.

7. *Comparisons:* We compare our weakest points to others' strongest points.

8. *Inability to say no:* failure to stand up for ourselves.

This is an extremely limited list of causes of a poor self-image. There are many others. But the point is, if we want to have our share of blue-ribbon days, we must recognize the problem, understand its cause, and then make an extreme effort to control it. If we cannot fix the problem, please, God, help us to adjust to it.

Self-image is the product of all our encounters plus our own reactions to these encounters. If we have traumatic experiences that cause us stress or experiences that question our integrity, our self-image is sure to suffer. We begin to question our worth or our ability to function acceptably.

MISTAKEN IDENTITY

My girls and I had had a busy day in early December of last year shopping, decorating the house, and visiting with friends. My son had been in a speech contest outside of Dallas that day and called about seven o'clock that night to say that they had won first place and he and his close friend Chad were celebrating at Chad's house. I quickly asked how they were planning to celebrate, and Brian responded, "We will rent a movie and order in pizza." They were extremely tired from the long day. Chad's parents said it was fine, so I consented. I asked Brian to call if they changed their plans. I did not hear from them, so I assumed they were okay.

We went to bed about eleven, and shortly thereafter, my doorbell rang. Isn't it amazing how many things rush through your mind as you wake up to a late-night ring, not knowing who is on the other side or why? I hurried to the door and looked through the peephole — directly into the eyes of a policeman. My heart stopped. The first thing that entered my mind was that something had happened to Brian. Had he been hurt? Or worse, had he been killed? I immediately opened the door, and the uniformed policeman introduced himself. He asked if I was Mrs. McCullough and if I had a son named Brian. I responded, "Yes."

He said, "Your son has been positively identified as vandalizing a home of its Christmas lights."

"Please come in, officer. How do you know it was my Brian?" I was flabbergasted.

"Is he tall? Does he wear glasses? Does he have a shiny jacket?" the officer asked.

"Yes...yes...yes.... But who told you he has done these things?"

"I cannot tell you, Mrs. McCullough, but he has been positively identified."

My heart sank, my lips quivered, and all the blood drained from my face. Then I said, "Who identified him?"

"I cannot tell you, Mrs. McCullough, but Brian will be prosecuted for this crime."

"Sir, let's go get Brian, and then I want the person who made the identification to face Brian and me and tell me."

I went to dress while the policeman called the police station to let them know that he was bringing in two boys — Brian McCullough, as the culprit, and Chad Smith, his accomplice. As I went down the hall to my bedroom, I thought, *What should I wear?* I was sure the *Dallas Morning News* would carry this story on the front page tomorrow under the headline: "Motivational Speaker's Son Jailed." I even imagined how I would look on the front page, so I decided I'd better wear something that made me look thin.

The officer put me in the back seat of the patrol car. When I looked on the computer screen next to the driver's seat and saw my son's name, BRIAN McCULLOUGH, I cannot tell you how I felt. We had called over to the Smiths' house and told Brian to get out of bed, because I was coming to get him. It was only a few blocks away but seemed like two hundred miles.

Mr. Smith, his son Chad, and Brian were dressed. The policeman explained to the boys about the accusations. I asked Brian if he had been out of the Smiths' home and he said, "No, Mom. I've been right here all evening, and I'd been asleep more than an hour when you called." I believed Brian and asked the officer if we could face the person accusing Brian and ask him to make a positive identification.

As I waited outside of the Smiths' house for them to come out, I felt so alone, but I knew that "God's in His heaven, and all's right with the world." I had to claim that promise at that time, no matter how bleak the night seemed. Then they all came out, and we got in the back seat of the patrol car.

My son was visibly shaking and continued to say, "Mama, I did not do it."

I answered, "Son, I know, but be patient. We will settle this shortly."

The alleged vandalizing had occurred only a few blocks away. We arrived, got out of the car, and walked the hundred-mile (well, it seemed that long!) walkway to the beautiful home. All five of us stood waiting for a response to the doorbell. A tall man came to the door. The officer introduced us, and immediately I said, "Is this the boy who vandalized your home?"

He replied, "No, I've never seen this young man before."

I said, "But you identified him; you sent the police over to my home, and it was called into the station that Brian McCullough was guilty of this."

He said, "I'm sorry, Mrs. McCullough, but these are not the boys who vandalized my lights." This man, this stranger, had seen a tall boy with glasses, wearing a shiny jacket, vandalizing his lights. The description fit Brian; someone had put a name together with a description, and the result was a false arrest.

Oh, what relief, joy, and so many other emotions engulfed me at that moment! I grabbed Brian, and we danced a jig. We both cried and hugged, cried and hugged.

Why do I tell you this story? Because this experience could have destroyed the self-image of a teenager — Brian. A humiliating brush with the law has affected many teenagers' lives. Only when you have a healthy self-image can you live up to your potential and *bee* all that you can *bee*.

Do not allow others to put an identity on you, except when you know that it is correct and true. There are many times in our lives when we lose our identities because of circumstances. For instance, as we marry, have children, or help our spouses in business, our identities may change over the years, depending on which role we're in. Then when the children are gone from home, we often realize that our identity no longer fits, and we wonder what our next identity will be — or if we'll have one at all! Sometimes we are caught up in trying to "wear too many hats." We have children, husbands, jobs, meals to prepare, clothes to wash, houses to clean, and many other "pulls," including meetings for school and the community. Is it any wonder that we feel we are "not together"? How can we be, when we are pulled in so many directions and have never learned to say "enough is enough"?

❤ • ❤ • ❤ • ❤ • ❤

HEARTITUDE

Don't Live a Mistaken Identity

❤ • ❤ • ❤ • ❤ • ❤

I speak from much experience, because I am as guilty as anyone in this area. When do we understand that we are not all things to all people? Each of us is only one, and we must clarify our own needs, along with those of family members and other people.

I would like to stress that this new decade is one in which we spread the work load around. We have to A-S-K to G-E-T. There is no written law anywhere that states that females have to do all the housework, for example. We all need to be conscious of the responsibilities of the home and share them. But sharing this responsibility often means we have to ask others to do their share.

As stated earlier, our identities will change throughout our lifetimes, and it is important to address those changes and make necessary adjustments. Hopefully, our identities will change for the better. If we continue to grow through life, then I guarantee you, our perceptions of ourselves will change upward.

And remember, the way we feel about ourselves and our identities has a direct bearing on how we treat others. This becomes apparent when we compare the typical characteristics of persons with high self-esteem and low self-esteem.

HIGH OR LOW SELF-ESTEEM

Person With High Self-Esteem:	Person With Low Self-Esteem:
Likes to think well of others	Likely to disapprove of others
Enjoys being with a large group	Uncomfortable when in groups
Comfortable when alone	Uncomfortable when alone Needs at least radio or TV for company
Expects to be accepted by others	Expects to be rejected by others
Evaluates self-worth as high	Evaluates self-worth as low
Does not mind being monitored by superiors	Is self-conscious and unable to function in presence of others
Able to defend himself or herself against negative comments	Has difficulty with negatives from others
Works well with superiors who demand high-quality work	Works well for less demanding superiors
Feels comfortable with management	Feels uneasy around management

COMPARE YOU TO YOU

Our self-images have been created by what has been said or not said to us, and what has been done to us and for us. It's tragic that many people never really realize their potential because they do not feel good about themselves. Compare yourself to you — not to others. Comparing yourself to others is like comparing a steak to a pizza: both are good but do not have the same ingredients or flavor. In their own way, each makes our world a little better place to work and live.

With a good self-image, each of us can do the same — contribute something to our world, our families, and our work. But without this strong self-image, we can easily become lost in an overwhelming sense of worthlessness, as this story by Jean Mizer illustrates:

> It started with tragedy on a biting cold February morning. I was driving behind the Milford Corners bus as I did most snowy mornings on my way to school. The bus veered and stopped short at the hotel, which it had no business doing, and I was annoyed as I had to come to an unexpected stop. A boy lurched out of the bus, reeled, stumbled, and collapsed on the snowbank at the curb. The bus driver and I reached him at the same moment. His thin, hollow face was white even against the snow.
>
> "He's dead," the driver whispered.
>
> It didn't register for a minute. I glanced quickly at scared young faces staring down at us from the school bus. "A doctor! Quick! I'll phone from the hotel...."
>
> "No use, I tell you he's dead." The driver looked down at the boy's still form. "He never even said he felt bad," he muttered. "Just tapped me on the shoulder and said, real quiet, 'I'm sorry. I have to get off at the hotel.' That's all. Polite and apologizing-like."
>
> At school, the giggling, shuffling morning noise quieted as the news went down the halls. I passed a huddle of girls. "Who was it? Who dropped dead on the way to school?" I heard one of them whisper.
>
> "Don't know his name; some kid from Milford Corners" was the reply.
>
> It was like that in the faculty room and the principal's office. "I'd appreciate your going out to tell the parents," the principal told me. "They haven't a phone and, anyway,

somebody from school should go there in person. I'll cover your classes."

"Why me?" I asked. "Wouldn't it be better if you did it?"

"I didn't know the boy," the principal admitted levelly. "And, in last year's sophomore personalities column I note that you were listed as his favorite teacher."

I drove through the snow and cold down the bad canyon road to the Evans place and thought about the boy, Cliff Evans. His favorite teacher! I thought. He hasn't spoken two words to me in two years! I could see him in my mind's eye, all right, sitting back there in the last seat in my afternoon literature class. He came in the room by himself and left by himself. "Cliff Evans," I muttered to myself, "a boy who never talked." I thought a minute. "A boy who never smiled. I never saw him smile once."

The big ranch kitchen was clean and warm. I blurted out my news somehow. Mrs. Evans reached blindly toward a chair. "He never said anything about bein' ailing."

His stepfather snorted. "He ain't' said nothin' about anything since I moved in here."

Mrs. Evans pushed a pan to the back of the stove and began to untie her apron. "Now hold on," her husband snapped. "I got to have breakfast before I go to town. Nothin' we can do now anyway. If Cliff hadn't been so dumb, he'd have told us he didn't feel good."

After school I sat in the office and stared blankly at the records spread out before me. I was to close the file and write the obituary for the school paper. The almost bare sheets mocked the effort. Cliff Evans, white, never legally adopted by stepfather, five young half-brothers and sisters. These meager strands of information and the list of D grades were all the records had to offer.

Cliff Evans had silently come in the school door in the mornings and gone out the school door in the evenings, and that was all. He had never belonged to a club. He had never played on a team. He had never held an office. As far as I could tell, he had never done one happy, noisy kid thing. He had never been anybody at all.

How do you go about making a boy into a zero? The grade-school records showed me. The first and second grade teachers' annotations read, "sweet, shy child," "timid but eager." Then the third grade note had opened the attack. Some teacher had written in a good, firm hand, "Cliff won't talk. Uncooperative. Slow learner." The other academic sheep had followed with "dull," "slow-witted," "low IQ." They became correct. The boy's IQ score in the ninth grade was listed as 83. But his IQ in the third grade had been 106. The score didn't go under 100 until the seventh grade. Even shy, timid, sweet children have resilience. It takes time to break them.

I stomped to the typewriter and wrote a savage report pointing out what education had done to Cliff Evans. I slapped a copy on the principal's desk and another in the sad, dog-eared file. I banged the typewriter and slammed the file and crashed the door shut, but I didn't feel much better. A little boy kept walking after me, a little boy with a peaked, pale face; a skinny body in faded jeans; and big eyes that had looked and searched for a long time and then had become veiled.

I could guess how many times he'd been chosen last to play sides in a game, how many whispered child conversations had excluded him, how many times he hadn't been asked. I could see and hear the faces and voices that said over and over, "You're a nothing, Cliff Evans."

A child is a believing creature. Cliff undoubtedly believed them. Suddenly it seemed clear to me: When finally there was nothing left at all for Cliff Evans, he collapsed on a snowbank and went away. The doctor might list "heart failure" as the cause of death, but that wouldn't change my mind.

We couldn't find ten students in the school who had known Cliff well enough to attend the funeral as his friends. So the student body officers and a committee from the junior class went as a group to the church, being politely sad. I attended the services with them, and sat through it with a lump of cold lead in my chest and a big resolve growing through me.

I've never forgotten Cliff Evans nor that resolve. He has been my challenge year after year, class after class. I look for veiled eyes or bodies scrounged into a seat in an alien world. "Look, kids," I say silently, "I may not do anything else for you this year, but not one of you is going to come out of here a nobody. I'll work or fight to the bitter end doing battle with society and the school board, but I won't have one of you coming out of here thinking himself a zero."

Most of the time — not always, but most of the time — I've succeeded.*

Every person is important and needs to be noticed and validated. It's so easy for us to love the lovely, but what about the unlovely? Cliff was one who was lost between the cracks. This story has been a reminder to me for years of the importance of every child and adult. Let's make a resolution not to lose one person — let us care for others as we would have them care for us.

---

*Jean Mizer, "Cipher in the Snow," from *Today's Education*, November 1964. Used by permission of Jean Todhunter Mizer and the National Education Association.

THE DAY I DISCOVERED
I HAD A GOOD, HEALTHY SELF-IMAGE

"As we imagine ourselves to be, so in time we will become." I had heard this quote many times in my life and had tried to visualize my life in ten, fifteen, and twenty years. I frankly had trouble doing this, so I faked it till I made it. I remember clearly when that day came, when faking it was no longer necessary.

In 1983, our church completed a multi-million-dollar building program. The big dedication day came. We were all so excited because a large number of "celebrities" were going to be in the service. My phone rang early that Sunday morning. It was my pastor. "Mamie, we are having a group for lunch today at Bent Tree County Club, and we would like to have you with us." Naturally, I said yes because I had always wanted to visit there. I had no idea who would be attending, but I was too busy to think about that. I had to get the children to church and taken care of while I attended the luncheon.

I arrived at Bent Tree, thank goodness, after all the other guests. I pulled up at the valet parking stand in my mud-speckled station wagon with my children's Sunday school pictures, Bibles, empty soft drink cans, and used Kleenex overflowing into the floorboard — a typical middle-class family wreck. I quickly tried to tidy up the car, left the keys with the parking attendant, and went into the beautiful building to ask where the luncheon was being held. Everyone was very cordial and gave me prompt directions.

Being the last one to arrive, I had a choice of one seat — between Mary Kay Ash of Mary Kay Cosmetics and George Beverly Shea of the Billy Graham Crusade. Across the table was Judge Abner McCall, president of Baylor University. All the other guests were just as impressive.

When the luncheon was over and I was driving home, I realized that I had been in "tall cotton" that day — and felt good about it. My car was several years old, and my suit was one of my "Nelly New" ensembles from a resale shop. However, none of that bothered me, and I realized for the first time, I felt good about being Mamie McCullough. I had not allowed anyone to make me feel inferior. I suppose for the first time I truly believed Eleanor Roosevelt's statement:

NO ONE CAN MAKE YOU FEEL INFERIOR WITHOUT YOUR PERMISSION.

Oh, what a relief it is. A good, healthy self-image is acquired through many small steps as we move toward the goal of being all that God wants us to *bee*.

GET IT TOGETHER — HERE'S HOW:

1. Everyone has talent and ability. If you want to *bee* original, *bee* yourself — you are special.

2. Keep in mind that you deserve the best that life can offer and whatever it is that you are willing to work for.

3. Remember: as we imagine ourselves to *bee,* so in time we will become.

4. Do not live a mistaken identity.

5. Spend more of your time building up others than tearing others down. Harsh words cannot be retracted any more than a bell can be unrung.

CHAPTER 5

DUST IS A PROTECTIVE COATING FOR FURNITURE

I believe that people should be our number one priority. I knew a young bride who would not develop any relationships in her community, her neighborhood, or her church because she was too busy: she had to clean her house every day. As she grew older, this priority remained. When she had children, her clean house came first with her. She didn't allow her family to enjoy their home, because it was a shrine to her housekeeping skills. She did not take the kids on picnics or go to their ball games; she did not take them fishing or to church.

❤ • ❤ • ❤ • ❤ • ❤

HEARTITUDE

Character Is Doing What Is Right — On Purpose

❤ • ❤ • ❤ • ❤ • ❤

The children are gone from home now, and she does not have those precious memories of sharing that home run, that first fish, a memorized Bible verse, her husband's hole-in-one on the golf course. Yes, her house is still clean and beautiful, but it is empty and lonesome now. She realized at last that family — not furniture — should have filled her days.

Where are our priorities? Do we dust the furniture instead of nurturing the people in our lives?

Sooner or later, each of us must address the question, "How shall I live my life?" Traditionally, early in our lives we try on many hats, trying to find out who we are and how we will live. We try one and fail; we try another and it doesn't fit; then we try and succeed, eventually finding a combination that works for us. It sometimes takes many years to arrive at a satisfactory lifestyle. One of the important factors in this process is setting priorities or goals.

What are your priorities in life? Many of us go through life adrift; we do not have a purpose. That is where goal-setting becomes helpful. I believe in big dreams of accomplishing great things. But we must have a plan, set goals and priorities, and not be distracted from our purpose as we make those dreams come true. It takes determination and perseverance to succeed; we must set our sails on a true course. If we determine that our goals are worth the work and sacrifice, we can move mountains.

In my opinion, the 1990s are a decade of family, home, church, education, commitment, loyalty, helping others, friends, and, yes, also of hard times. We will be better able to cope with our difficulties, because in this decade we will bind together as families and friends, propping each other up, and making each other stronger. We will encourage others to reach out more, not just to "touch someone," as the telephone ad used to say, but also to help each other.

We've all heard the saying, "We only go around once in life." But that's okay. If we do it right, once is enough. Whether we are dealing with religion, family, or career, doing it right means we need to set some priorities early in our lives. The earlier in life we decide how we are going to live, the fewer frustrations we will encounter. And we also need to remember that character is doing what is right, on purpose.

Many very successful corporations have prospered under strong leaders who based their priorities on Christian principles. Two of my favorite examples are Mary Crowley, who built Home Interiors, and Mary Kay Ash, of Mary Kay Cosmetics. Both women espoused the priorities of God first, family second, and business or career third.

When I was a part-time independent sales consultant for Mary Kay Cosmetics, I also had a full-time teaching job and was mother of three children, all under four years of age. My days and nights were busy, busy, busy; but I worked hard at keeping my priorities in order.

One of the "memories" my children still talk about is what we did when I would unpack a Mary Kay order. They would take the nice pink boxes and stack them to make the Eiffel Tower, the Empire State Building, London Bridge, or whatever they wanted the boxes to be. As I called customers and booked shows, they played in and around my desk.

These types of working conditions might have been a terrible inconvenience for some people, but we knew they were necessary, so we made the most of just being together. We do not always have to be looking directly at our children and spouse for them to know that we care about them. My children and I enjoyed these good "growing times" together!

Most women are out of the home because of necessity, not because they want to "dress up and be seen," as I have heard women's careers explained. I must admit that the reason I have been in the working world since I was eight years old is because of necessity, not because I wanted to work long, hard hours. While in college, I worked four jobs just to provide the necessities.

FIND A WAY, OR MAKE ONE

We work also to make a life for our families and to help provide the things necessary to give our children opportunities which some of us were not fortunate enough to have. There were times in my life when I worked with my children under foot and times when I had to work two jobs. My husband lost his job at one point, and I was forced into working still harder.

Some people are quick to judge us when they think we have our priorities out of line. I worked because I had to, but I always put love of home and family above love of career.

As I said earlier, there have been times in my life when I've been accused of being a perfectionist. And there were times when that extended to my house. Clutter, dust, dirt, or light switches surrounded by small fingerprints were not to be endured.

But as my schedule has filled with traveling and writing, as well as mothering, I've changed my priorities to recognize what's really important in my life. And what's important are my beliefs, my family, and my work. This has led me to develop a new, more tolerant attitude toward household dirt and clutter. In fact, I've sort of come to appreciate dust; I have decided it serves as a protective coating for my furniture — and with a family like mine, my furniture needs all the protection it can get!

Even though I joke about housework, I really do enjoy cooking for my family and friends. To cook for twenty-five folks for Sunday dinner is a treat. This is like therapy to me. My mission in life has changed through the years. I feel that God has called me to *bee* several things: a mother, a friend, a speaker, and an author. He has made it clear that what I must do to help others is to speak and write. I hope and pray when I take my last breath on this earth that I hear the words, "Well done, my good and faithful servant." That will be my reward for having the right priorities and living a fruitful and productive life for all the right reasons.

SPIRITUAL PRIORITIES

As I spoke recently to a group of graduating seniors in Cleburne, Texas, my goal was to challenge these youth. Because I usually speak anywhere from one hour to three days, it was difficult for me to have only twenty minutes to deliver this challenge. After reading Dr. Jay Strack's book, *Aim High*, I decided to use "Aim High" for the title of my challenge. Using ideas from his book, I tried to cut the speech to only three points. You see, we Baptists always have three points and a poem in each sermon.

1. Build a strong foundation on Biblical principles.

2. Have and maintain a clear set of moral values.

3. Decide how you will live your life; then get busy living it. Success is a continuous effort. We never get to let up; *today* is all we have. We do not succeed on yesterday's laurels.

My pastor, Dr. Jack Graham, related a story recently which said a lot about how we set our spiritual priorities. He asked how many of us believed everything we read in the daily newspapers. No one raised a hand. Then he asked how many of us believed everything we read in the Bible. All hands went up. He said, "Why, then, do we spend so much time reading something we do not believe and so little time on what we do believe?" Good question, isn't it? Setting priorities helps us remember what's really important. With our priorities in place, we're better able to "keep the main thing the main thing."

Martin Luther King, Jr., said, "We must accept finite disappointment, but we must never lose infinite hope." We never get too much hope, and we can get a daily dose of it directly from the Bible. Be as consistent as possible in getting your spiritual priorities in order, and include plenty of exposure to God's Word. We need to spread the word so we can continue to grow spiritually. (This action will indeed keep some WD-40 on our hopeometers!)

We also continue to grow through associating with people we would like to emulate. As you consider spiritual priorities, choose some spiritual mentors who can challenge and encourage you. There is nothing wrong with copying other people. This practice helps us grow spiritually, mentally, and emotionally.

I've even chosen an insect as something to admire and emulate. The bumblebee is a symbol of encouragement which I learned about some fifteen years ago. Since that time, I have heard that Napoleon was the first person recorded to have used the bumblebee as a symbol, placing one on the front of each of his soldiers' helmets.

Its significance? It has been said that the bumblebee cannot fly: its wings are too light and its body too heavy. However, the bee doesn't know that, so he flies.

❤ • ❤ • ❤ • ❤ • ❤

HEARTITUDE

Keep the Main Thing the Main Thing

❤ • ❤ • ❤ • ❤ • ❤

As you learned in the Introduction to this book, I have used the bee as my symbol to remind others that "you can *bee* what you want to *bee*." It is God's plan in each of our lives to use our time and talents to *bee* the best we can. Oftentimes, a person will ask me why I have the bee pinned on my shoulder. Sometimes they seem to think that perhaps I do not know it is there. "Do you know you have a bee on your shoulder?" they ask. I reply, "It is better than a chip." Then I quickly tell them the Napoleon story and, if possible, ask them if they "*bee*lieve," taking this time to witness and share the Gospel.

SETTING PRIORITIES

I realize that I am old-fashioned, but my family is very high on my list of priorities. In the '80's, family life took a beating, and I believe the deterioration of the family is largely responsible for the deterioration of our society. What is a family? According to the New York Supreme Court decision of 1989, the following constitutes a family:

> *two adult lifetime partners whose relationship is long-term and characterized by an emotional and financial commitment and inter-dependence, or*
> *two homosexuals, or*
> *two unmarried heterosexuals, or*
> *three or four adults who live together.*

According to the Bureau of Vital Statistics in Washington, D.C., only six percent of households are made up of a working dad and a housewife at home with two children. In 1990, half of all American families were headed by a single parent. Other family trends for the '90's include:

1. More "double-duty" caregivers for dependent kids and the elderly will be needed.

2. There will be more minority, middle-class families.

3. The fastest-growing homeless group will be comprised of families with children and one full-time worker (whose average income is $7,200 per year).

4. Most dependent care will be given not by agencies or government, but by families.

5. Most women with children will be working either outside the home or in sales, or with computers in the home.

6. Quality childcare will be recognized as being vital for families.

7. Of kids raised by their mother, 38 percent will never see their father.

8. Most kids will not be from "traditional" families.

9. Seven million kids ages ten through seventeen will be at "high risk" of delinquency, drug abuse, school failure, or teen pregnancy.

These are alarming statistics for a nation that was built on the traditional family cornerstone. They have made me even more determined to set a priority of spending quality and quantity time listening to my kids, believing them, and encouraging them. Here's one example of how this has paid off.

My son, Brian, was twelve in March, 1987. At that time he was not interested in things pertaining to cleaning his room. His interest lay in outdoor activities and sports (anything outside the house!). His idea of a cleaned room was one in which the bed and cover were in the same room.

Our good friends from Oklahoma, Mike and Jan Fry and son Steven, visited our home that year during spring break. The men had planned to play golf, but just as they were ready to leave, one of those terrible Texas spring storms hit with lots of wind, heavy rains, lightning, and thunder. This canceled their golf game.

Steven suggested that since they could not go to the club to play, perhaps they should clean Brian's room for something to do. I quickly said, "Yes!" After breakfast, Brian and Steven went into his bedroom and began. They closed the door and immediately began to laugh and seemed to be having quite a good time. Patti, then fourteen, and Jennifer, ten, decided to join the boys for the cleanup. Now there were four young people in that one bedroom, and the noise level was growing. I went to the door and knocked. The only answer, however, was, "Wait until we finish and we'll explain."

They were in the room most of the day. Once in awhile one of them would come through with a bag of throwaways and would always be giggling. My curiosity and suspicions grew. I asked several times what they were doing and finding. Still the only answer I got was, "Wait 'til supper, Mom. Brian will explain." I could not imagine what they had found and wondered why they would not tell me.

Now, you have to understand something about me — I'm a worrier, and for your information, worrying works, because everything I've ever worried about has never happened. So it has to work.

I prodded each child to give me a hint of what the excitement was, but no one would give me a clue. Supper finally came and when we finished, the children said, "Mama, Brian wants to explain what we found in his room."

Brian never looked worried or upset about having to explain what they had found. In fact, I was probably more nervous than he was. I was "under the gun" because Steven's father was a superintendent of schools in Oklahoma, and I had done six years of in-service work for his faculty. They knew what I espoused from the podium. Secretly, I had an uneasy feeling that I was about to be discredited.

Patti said, "Mama, we found three things in Brian's room that we do not think he can explain."

Jennifer added, "We found a long-handled pair of pruning shears under Brian's bed."

To which Brian quickly retorted, "Mama, it's your fault." (Now, tell me, do children come into this world saying "it's somebody else's fault"?) "Mama, don't you remember three months ago when you told me to cut the limbs off the tree outside my window?"

I did. "But how did the shears get under the bed?"

He said, "I took the shears from the garage, went through the house, opened the window, clipped the limbs, shut the window, and left the shears on the window sill. I guess they just slid down behind the bed."

I believe that, don't you? Say yes....

"What about the other items?" I prodded.

Patti said, "Mama, I'm so mad at Brian because I have been looking for this miniskirt for weeks, and all the time it was under his bed." I cannot tell you what thoughts I had at that moment. A miniskirt? Be real. Not Brian — my son — never!

He quickly retorted. "It's Patti's fault. Don't you all remember several months ago we were invited to the Patrick O'Dooleys' for Sunday dinner and we took sweats to change into to play basketball?" We all remembered. "Well," Brian said, "Patti put her skirt in my duffel bag to bring home. When we got home she didn't take it out or come get it, so I just kicked it under the bed so I wouldn't have to look at it."

I believe that, don't you? Say yes....

I realized they were saving the worst for last. Patti said, "Brian cannot explain this one, I am sure."

Brian began to explain that he surely did not want me to be mad at him for this. He said, "Mama, when you are out of town sometimes, the girls and I fight."

I suppose he thought that would be a big surprise to me. I said, "What has that got to do with what they found under your bed?"

He said, "The third thing they found was a pair of pantyhose."

Don, the children's father, had taught me to respond, not to react, so I said calmly, "Brian, help me understand why the pantyhose were under your bed."

Have you ever had a time when your entire life passed before you? This was one of those times. I imagined him coming down my hall in high heels, hose, and a wig....Oh, no!

He quickly explained that when I'm out of town, Patti and Jennifer gang up on him. (He seemed to think that mothers don't realize what goes on behind their backs.) He said when they make him mad, he takes the pair of pantyhose and puts tennis balls in each of the legs and twirls them around and hits the girls. You see, he was using the pantyhose as a weapon.

I believe that, don't you? Say yes....

Just think what might have happened if I had found the pruning shears, miniskirt, and pantyhose under Brian's bed and had not taken the time to listen and had assumed the wrong thing. I could have taken Brian to the best psychologist in Dallas and spent thousands of dollars and still not have known what the real motive was. We must listen and allow others to explain, because their reasons for doing things are never the same as what we might assume.

❤ • ❤ • ❤ • ❤ • ❤

HEARTITUDE

Good listening should be a priority for us. It is not just a means of communication. It is a gift, an act of love.

Listening Is Loving

And it's a useful skill outside the home too. As Calvin Coolidge said, "No one ever listened himself out of a job."

❤ • ❤ • ❤ • ❤ • ❤

DO UNTO OTHERS

Another priority for me is helping others, even though I know helping people is not always an easy task. Many of us want to help but are not creative enough to know how to go about it. Recently, I was told of a fire in my neighborhood in which the unfortunate family lost most of their household goods. Neighbors fretted about what was best to do and how to help; no one could decide on a course of action. While they were deliberating on what to do, a young man of modest means had a lounge chair and a TV set delivered to the victims' temporary dwelling. Didn't this man show uncommon generosity? He helped in the best way he could think of. As you've already heard me say, start. Any gesture of kindness, I believe, is taken in good faith.

We must remember also that people need help when they need it, not necessarily when it is convenient for us to give it. We must help others on their time schedules, not just when we have nothing else to do. Help at the wrong time is no help at all. Perhaps it is your spouse wanting to relate the day's activities, a child who's eager to share his or her excitement about a good grade, or an employee who simply needs to let you know his or her situation. Try to give your attention when it's most needed and most beneficial. If possible, give it when it's requested, and try to avoid saying, "Not now." Remember, listening is loving.

GET IT TOGETHER — HERE'S HOW:

1. Build a foundation on strong principles. Decide what priorities you intend to live by. Decide these principles early in life and build every decision based on them.

2. Keep the main thing the main thing. We often quit too soon because we lose the dream of the big picture.

3. It's always right to do right. On the other hand, the "right" to do something doesn't always make it the right thing to do. No matter what decision we make — whether in family or career — it is always right to do right. That is a given.

4. Find the best way to help provide for you and your family. All family members should know what we do and why.

5. Develop your listening skills through practice. Listening is truly loving and caring for others.

Chapter 6

Let Paper Remember So You Can Forget

The reward of a thing well done is to have done it.
—*Ralph Waldo Emerson*

This did not really happen, but fantasize with me:

One cold winter night in January, friends from Georgia dropped in on us unexpectedly. They were on a business trip to Dallas and decided that they had time for an overnight visit. We were thrilled to see our old friends. We would have a wonderful time hearing about what was going on in Georgia. It didn't occur to me until later that my kitchen was completely bare of the common breakfast essentials. No problem. I would send Brian to the grocery store to get some items for breakfast: ham, oatmeal, milk, and eggs.

"Don't forget, Brian — ham, oatmeal, milk, and eggs," I said. "You can remember by H O M E — ham, oatmeal, milk, and eggs."

Well, Brian went to the store, and he remembered H O M E but returned with honey, olives, mushrooms, and escargot! Escargot for breakfast? What kind of breakfast is that? Here I am with a house full of company and I have nothing but escargot to serve for breakfast. Panic. Crisis. Calamity.

Oh, what we do to ourselves in a situation that has no importance at all! Now, years later, what difference did it make that we had a bizarre epicurean breakfast?

♥ • ♥ • ♥ • ♥ • ♥

HEARTITUDE

The Faintest Ink Is Better Than the Most Retentive Memory

♥ • ♥ • ♥ • ♥ • ♥

This is one of my favorite stories; it pictures a frustration, a hassle, a really stressful situation. It is the kind of situation that causes my blood pressure to go sky high. Do you know the feeling? Now, how can we help ourselves out of such stressful experiences?

There are some simple, small steps that we — you and I — can take to help ourselves. Why didn't I make a list for Brian? A simple grocery list can prevent three extra trips to town and a lot of stress. A little thing? Yes, a little mistake, a little frustration — but after all, aren't the little things the ones that push us over the brink?

I included this imaginary situation simply to serve as a reminder that making a list — a little list — can prevent a big frustration. And anything that prevents a frustration or a hassle is worth a try. *Let paper remember....*

Make a list. Think on paper. Take notes so you won't lose your best ideas. Writing was invented to preserve the great thoughts of mankind. The written word solves problems, answers questions, settles disputes, proves equations, confirms agreements, resolves issues, and stores information. We should never trust important matters to memory. The faintest ink is better than the most retentive memory. *Let paper remember....*

President George Bush knows how to use the pencil to remember. Lovely Barbara Bush tells that on the day that her husband was to become the forty-first president, the sixty-four-year-old Bush apparently held fast to the schedule he had scribbled on a note pad for his press secretary:

> 6 A.M. — Catch three news shows
>
> Drink coffee
>
> Play with grandkids
>
> Go to White House
>
> Go to Cap. Hill
>
> Get sworn in*

Let paper remember....

---

*Reported in *Saturday Oklahoman and Times,* January 21, 1989.

Have a plan every day; write it down on paper. Write down what *must* be done at the top of the list, what *could* be done next, and finally what *might* be done. Sue Davis, a teacher friend of mine, once told me that she would rather face a firing squad than to face a classroom full of students, if she did not have a solid plan of action for that school day. Not only that, she suggested having enough plans for two days — just in case.

Keep your written plan visible at all times, and mark off each item as it is completed. What a sense of accomplishment! Even a small success becomes a victory.

Let paper remember....

SIMPLIFY, SIMPLIFY, SIMPLIFY

Henry David Thoreau taught us to simplify our lives. He went to the woods for two years and lived beside Walden Pond to see how simply he could live his life. He believed that if one had more concerns than could be counted on ten fingers, that person's life was too complicated. He believed one should be able to keep all accounts on a thumbnail. (Good-bye, accountants!) He taught: instead of three meals, eat one. (Good-bye, Slim-Fast!) Can you imagine how much time and money we would conserve if we ate only one meal a day?

These ideas might have worked in the nineteenth century, but they are unrealistic today. Nevertheless, the suggestion to simplify our lives is still valid. We live in a complicated world; a fast, high-tech world. We hold down jobs, we raise families, we get caught in traffic, we support our churches, we manage households. No wonder we live under such stress. No wonder the newspapers are full of horrible suicide stories. No wonder we buckle under the pressure. No wonder we occasionally ask, "Am I going to make it?"

Yes, yes, you *can* make it! You can make it if you simplify your life. Follow Thoreau's advice: simplify, simplify, simplify. Do those things that will make a difference in your life and eliminate others. Cut out the deadwood. "Genius is the ability to reduce the complicated to the simple," wrote C. W. Cerar. This statement remains eternally true.

One way to simplify our lives is to learn to organize and manage our time. Time is a valuable commodity. Treat it with respect; save it or use it, but use it wisely. Did you ever stop to think that we all have the same amount of time given to us every day — twenty-four hours? The president of the United States, corporate leaders, salespersons, teachers, students — all have the same amount of time. Everybody has the same twenty-four hours, and yet there are those who seem to have plenty of time for everything, with time left over, while many others have to say, "I would like to do that, but I just don't have the time."

Be clock-conscious. Set your watch five minutes ahead; it will make you conscious of time, and it will keep you punctual. (*Bee* there and *bee* on time.) But don't be a clock watcher; clock watching is a negative action. Did you ever stop to think that when you look at your watch, you are looking at passed time? If my watch reads eight o'clock, that means that eight hours have passed out of my lifetime — eight hours that I will never get to spend again. Did I use those hours well? Don't be a clock watcher; be a *time* watcher.

DECIDE AND DO IT

Block out chunks of time for big jobs. There is nothing as frustrating as an unfinished job. Determine the time of day that you work best and do the hard jobs, the demanding jobs, the unpleasant jobs first. Finish the jobs you begin — if they are worth finishing. Every job we begin is not a worthy project, but if it is, finish the task as soon as possible and get it behind you. As W. M. Jones noted, "Nothing is so fatiguing as the eternal hanging on of an uncompleted task."

In managing our time, we should attempt to control technology. Have you seen the cartoon of the cowboy on a runaway horse — hair flying, feet out of the stirrups, chaps askew? The caption says, "It's okay; I'm in complete control!" That is about how we all control technology.

We love those fancy gadgets. I have a new computer, and I find myself sitting and staring at the screen for hours. It is a monster that I resolve to conquer, but in the meantime it eats up my time. I have converted my garage into an office, with three new mind-boggling telephones that have me hanging up on friends, transferring calls to Australia, and putting the police on hold — all of which must be corrected at a tremendous loss of time. Even the television robs me. How often have I watched shows that were a complete waste of time? Don't misunderstand, TV is a marvelous device, but sometimes I would be better off mowing the grass.

Yes, we must learn to control technology. And in order to survive, we must be willing to be flexible in an ever-changing world. I resisted learning the computer, because I did not feel it was necessary. Ha! Was I ever wrong! How exciting this decade is because of all the new technology!

Even when we are in complete control, we all experience failures. Forget them — they cannot be changed. Time spent on regrets is time wasted. Go on to new and worthier endeavors. Often a very thin line separates a success from a failure or a loss from a win. Have you ever noticed how many times a basketball game has been won by a score of 123 to 122 or some other such margin? A horse race by a tenth of a second? A football game by a point after a touchdown? In these cases you do not have winners and losers — you have those who had the highest score and those who were right behind them.

Ninety-nine percent of us will not be number one, but that does not mean we are losers. We can be winners whether we are number one or not. I am a winner and you are too!

ALL DECISIONS ARE NOT CREATED EQUAL

Decision making is a learned skill, and one that needs endless practice. When the occasion calls for a decision, make it. Never leave a decision unresolved. Some decisions are important enough that they affect our entire lives: decisions about careers, education, marriage, religion, childbearing. These are the decisions that take much consideration and counseling. They are arrived at after much thought, prayer, discussion, and much soul-searching.

None of these decisions should be taken lightly. Not only do they affect us, but they affect our whole circle of family and friends as well. I have heard some people say, after making an unfortunate decision, "Oh, well, I am not hurting anybody but myself." How far from the truth that is! When we hurt, others hurt too. Not only do the ones who love us hurt with us, but often those people are involved directly or indirectly in the consequences of the action. On the other hand, do not spend endless time on decisions that have little consequence: What shall I wear? What television show shall I watch? Where shall I eat? What shall I order?

Have you ever tied up the line at McDonald's for five minutes while you decided between a Big Mac or a Quarter Pounder? Make a choice and live with it; don't agonize over it, and don't continue to vacillate from one response to the other.

In hard decisions, the best first response is no, because it is easier to change from no to yes than it is to switch from yes to no. Yes opens the floodgates that are hard to shut off if the need arises, while people are often happy when one slides from no to yes.

Some decisions can be made once and for all and won't have to be addressed again. Isn't it wonderful when the agony is over and the answer is ready? For instance, if the decision is made early in the life of a family that the family will go to church every Sunday, then that is a decision that will not have to be debated every Saturday night. If the decision is made that the children will not spend the night with a friend during the week, that decision will never have to be made again. Early on I decided that, no matter what, my children would never own a motorcycle, as least as long as they lived under my roof. That is one decision that I will never have to face again. It was made, once and for all, a long time ago.

LEARN TO SAY NO

As we're learning to manage our time and committing our priorities to paper, we must learn to say no. Be gracious, but learn to say it. Nothing is more frustrating than taking on too many jobs, trying to accomplish a daily list of tasks that *no one* could do in a day. Of course, those who are looking for help seek out the doers, the achievers, the I CAN people. You are one of these people, but you cannot be all things to all people; you cannot do everything for everybody who asks.

Decide where your talents and interests lie, choose what you wish to work on, find your mission, and say no to the other requests. Be gracious, but say no. We have a choice, and we owe no excuses for the choices we make. And don't let someone who is requesting a favor of you make you feel guilty if your answer is no. Years ago, I learned to say no when I heard of someone who refused in this manner: "That sounds like a wonderful project, a really worthwhile undertaking. I appreciate so much your wanting me to be a part of it. For a number of reasons I cannot accept, but I thank you for inviting my help." No one could be offended by such a gracious refusal.

When you learn to say no, you will have less chance of getting caught in the empty-bucket syndrome. You are the bucket and every time you do something for someone, you give away a part of yourself. This can be a good thing, of course. But unless you learn to say no, you will soon come up empty, too exhausted and frustrated to do anything for anybody — even yourself.

I have taught school, and on occasion I have come home completely sapped, completely worn out, completely exhausted; my bucket was often empty. Every person I came in contact with seemed to take a dip out of my bucket. *Dip, dip, dip.* In fact, I remember coming home so depleted I did not even want music. I told my husband, "Unplug the refrigerator — it's too loud." I had not said no; I had let everyone dip from my bucket until there was absolutely nothing left! The superintendent needed a letter edited; the accountant needed to check the senior class bank statement; the principal wanted someone to cover a third period class for a sick teacher; the coach wanted a tutor for a failing athlete; a student needed help on a research theme. *Dip, dip, dip.*

Schoolteachers are not the only ones who sometimes have empty buckets. You secretaries, you doctors, you carpenters, you single parents, you hairdressers — all of you know what I am talking about. *Dip, dip, dip.* Why do we let ourselves become empty? This is another one of those things that get the best of us.

Take a small step. Say no to some of these demands. When your bucket is empty, you are no good to yourself or to anyone else. I read in the *Dear Abby* column that no one can take advantage of you without your permission. How true! Save some time every day for yourself; schedule it in and do not let anything interfere with this time of rest and recreation. Even a hot bath behind a locked bathroom door would be acceptable.

One of the reasons that I feel so strongly about resting is that for years I did not really know what it was to take time off and rest. I never saw myself as a workaholic, but I think other people did. I always thought I had to work, because I had to make a living. After I had my last baby, I had to go back to work in two weeks because we had to have groceries, make house payments, and help my mother. I had no choice but to work. Now, however, I'm a little bit wiser and a little bit more experienced. I know that I have to make myself rest, because I have discovered that when I don't, little problems are compounded into bad situations. I've noticed in raising my three children that when they are tired, everything is wrong; their hair doesn't do right, the food tastes bad, the shirts have wrinkles — everything is wrong. But when we feel rested, these little annoyances seem hardly worth noticing.

When we're tired, we not only let little irritations become big problems, we also are more vulnerable to letting others dictate our attitudes. The slightest snub, the smallest remark, can send us into a swirling tornado of anger when we're tired, while the same remark might seem funny when we're refreshed.

This really came home to me recently. I serve on a board for dropout kids in Dallas. The administrator called and asked if I would meet with a group at 6 a.m. on the other end of Dallas for a briefing on some materials. Of course, trying to be a good board member, I said yes. *Dip, dip, dip.* So I got up that morning about 4:30 a.m. It was cold and rainy. I dressed and went all the way across Dallas. We had a wonderful meeting.

It was still raining about eight o'clock when we finished. We were on the side of Dallas where I visit an eighty-eight-year-old woman in a retirement center, so I thought, *I'll just go by and see her; I'll kill two birds with one stone.* I had not seen this lady for probably ten days, so I stopped by one of the stores and purchased some flowers, thinking it would cheer her up and make me feel good also. I got to the retirement center, and I couldn't find her, so I visited with people up and down the hall, but I never did find my friend. Oh, well....

I started home. Then I noticed that I didn't have any gas, and you must know this was in a part of Dallas where I really didn't feel comfortable pumping gasoline, but I had no choice. I got out in the rain, pumped the gas, and ran in to give the service station man my credit card. As he was processing the charge, here came this man from a topless bar across the street, carrying a can of beer in his hand. He asked the clerk to call him a cab. I was trying to stay out of the way and be as inconspicuous as possible, but being almost six feet tall, I often find it difficult to be inconspicuous.

As I was attempting to get the clerk to hurry and give me my ticket so that I could get out of there, the man looked at me and said, "I bet I know how old you are." I didn't look at him because I did not think he was talking to me. Then he said, "But you're not my type."

I realized then that he was standing near me and that indeed he was addressing me. I said, "Are you talking to me?"

"Yeah, you don't look too bad for your age, but you're just not my type." I still know how old you are. You're fifty-six years old."

Fifty-six years old! I want you to know that I had just turned fifty. Now there is nothing wrong with being fifty-six, but when you are fifty, looking like you are fifty-six is not a priority. I just stood and glared at him.

He persisted in his drunken, slurring words, "But you do look pretty good for a fifty-six-year-old woman. I'm just forty-six myself." I thought, *You're the one who looks fifty-six!*

I was still trying to get out of the store when he said, "And another thing. I just want to tell you that for fifty-six you look pretty good and I'm just sorry you're not my type."

I had had just about all of this I could stand. Have you ever been in it up to your eyeballs? This was one of those times for me. Here I had been trying to be a good citizen — doing what I was supposed to be doing, helping the dropout kids and visiting the retirement center. I just didn't deserve this aggravation.

I froze that drunk with one last glance, and he said, "I'm pretty smart, don't you think?"

I lost my patience at that. "No, sir, you're not very smart because you have just insulted a fifty-year-old woman and if you were very smart you wouldn't have done that because I'm going out to get in a brand new car and you have to call a cab!" What I really wanted to do was to stomp his foot and say, "Not only can you not think, but you can't walk either!"

This encounter bothered me all day; a strange man, a drunk, told me I looked fifty-six years old. Why would a thing like that bother a sensible, fifty-year-old woman? Because I was tired — worn out from the 4:30 a.m. wakeup, the drive across Dallas on rain-slick streets, the frustration of being unable to find my friend in the nursing home, and the discomfort of having to get out of my car and pump gas in a rather dangerous part of town. (Not to mention the fact that I was only fifty!)

The point I am making is this: when we are tired and upset, every-thing gets on our nerves. So sort your priorities, make your list, and make sure you schedule time for yourself. Then go get in that tub of hot water.

ORGANIZE IN SMALL STEPS
☙

The word *organize* has a way of intimidating some people. These people aren't organized; they realize organization is desirable, but they don't know how to go about putting it into their everyday lives. If you have no organizational skills, begin with a small, simple step. (Remember, even small steps can cover great distances.) Get a loose-leaf binder — a worn-out Mickey Mouse notebook discarded by the kids will be fine. Separate the notebook into sections with dividers, tab them with items that you need to keep track of, and arrange them in the appropriate sections: telephone numbers, Christmas card addresses, medical appointments, regular meetings, correspondence, bills to be paid, receipts, home repairs, prescriptions, favorite recipes — the list is endless. As you begin taking care of these things systematically, organization becomes a habit; it is fun to see things fall into place, and to be able to find all those items that seemed to get permanently lost when you habitually put them under the sugar bowl.

Then when organization seems less of a threat, we can venture into some other places where this habit pays off. Where are your keys? Your sunglasses? Your purse? If you will have a special place to put those things that we all traditionally misplace, you will always know where to look for them. Here are some suggestions: When you come into the house, hang your car keys on a special peg — every time. Put your sunglasses in a special drawer — every time. Put your purse under the bed — every time. Then when you need your keys, your sunglasses, or your purse, you will know exactly where they are — every time.

As you continue to see what a time-saver and nerve-saver your organizational skills have become, you will be challenged to put order into the other areas of your life. Organization does not mean that your life or your house or your workplace is perfectly straight and orderly at all times. This is not realistic, considering the pace of our lives, nor should it be. We must avoid unrealistic standards of perfection, because none of us is perfect. To spend endless hours polishing a project just to achieve perfection is not time-effective. In fact, some jobs are best to be "quick and dirty." Sir Simon Marks, chairman of Great Britain's highly successful retail chain of Marks & Spencer, is reported to have said, "The price of perfection is prohibitive."

Getting organized can get us started on the road to being all that God intended us to *bee*. And we can start on our goal of organization by sorting our priorities, then committing to paper the things we hope to accomplish each and every day. It is a small beginning, but one that can help us accomplish big things.

Let paper remember....

GET IT TOGETHER — HERE'S HOW:

1. Let paper remember so you can forget. Write it down.

2. Simplify your life by using organizational skills.

3. Practice making decisions. Spend time and prayer on the critical decision, and don't agonize over the trivial ones.

4. Learn to say no. If you let them, people will keep your bucket dry.

5. Make a decision early in your life about standards, principles, and values, and try to live by them. Decide how you'll live and do it.

6. Remember that little things make the big difference in life.

CHAPTER 7

POSITIVE DOING

*Wantivation is the art of encouraging others with a plan
as well as the desire to act upon a better way of life.*

—*Mamie McCullough*

Wantivation — never heard that word, have you?

Wantivation is a word I made up. My friends do not always understand what I am talking about when I use it, but the meaning is perfectly clear to me. Let me try to explain it to you. I was a schoolteacher, and all teachers know how important it is to define terms. Unless we are all tuned in to the same meanings, there is a terrible communication gap. *Wantivation* is a combination of the words *want* and *motivation*. Who understands the meaning of *want?* Raise your hands. Yes, we know that word — we learned it early. Are you a parent? If so, you hear the word frequently. And that's okay. If we don't want anything (out of life, for instance), we become complacent, satisfied, static. We need to want. But, more importantly, we need to control our wants and direct them into productive channels.

> ❤ • ❤ • ❤ • ❤ • ❤
>
> HEARTITUDE
>
> *A Smile Not Shared Enlarges and Settles in Your Hips*
>
> ❤ • ❤ • ❤ • ❤ • ❤

Now, let's consider the word *motivation.* I am a motivational speaker and a motivational writer. My heartfelt desire is to motivate others to *bee* better, to live a better life, to get it together. *Wantivation* is helping others to dream and set goals, encouraging them to start achieving those goals, finding the positive approach to all situations, and learning to share with others the I CAN way of life.

I invented that word a long time ago when I was a little girl in Dixie, Georgia. I remember sitting on the porch step, wanting to be better. This memory embodies the two ingredients of *wantivation:* an intense wanting plus a worthwhile goal. That brings us to the conclusion that *wantivation* requires positive action. Everybody wants, but wanting is a hollow activity if we do not follow it with a positive plan of actually doing something to achieve what we want.

If a person is to make a life of positive doing, he or she must have a positive attitude. Attitude is so important that I cannot stress it enough. Many more jobs are lost because of attitude and failure to get along with people than because of poor skills. Positive personal relationships cannot exist unless the attitudes are right. To paraphrase a familiar adage, you can accomplish more with honey than you can with vinegar. That doesn't mean we should fawn or be subservient. It simply means that we should treat others as we would like to be treated.

If your attitude is bad, change it! Grit your teeth and just do it. You must have a positive, cheerful attitude, but be sure you are sincere — people sense it when you are putting on. And try putting some gratitude in your attitude.

WHAT THE MIND
HARBORS, THE BODY MANIFESTS

Your attitude shows up in what you say and how you say it. To be a positive doer, start by eliminating five words from your vocabulary:

1. *Can't.* We must learn how to be "I CAN" people instead of "I CAN'T" people. In 1974 when I was teaching high school business law students, I decided that I would try to use something tangible to help the students understand how important the I CAN concept would be in their future. Having been in the business world for many years and having hired numerous types of personnel, I would find myself thinking, *Why don't these people know the value of saying "I can" or "I'll try"?*

I asked the students what an I CAN'T looked like. I said, "You are always using that word; tell me the shape, size, and color of an I CAN'T." They looked at me with that "Teacher, be real" look. I responded, "Okay, if you cannot tell me what an I CAN'T looks like by tomorrow, bring me a tin can."

Their look of shock and dismay was quite evident. The next morning they all appeared in my class with tin cans. Some were large, some were fat, some were skinny. They each had a can, and each can was different. Suddenly I perceived visually how different and unique each child was. Each had different talents and abilities — and I, the teacher, had to teach them as a class. That is why I have such a special affinity for educators: I realize the tremendous job they have — daily.

The students were actually excited about what I was going to do with the cans. I had cut pictures of eyes out of old magazines, and I gave one to each student. "You couldn't tell me what an I CAN'T is, so I'm going to show you something that you might find a whole lot more useful," I said. "When you take an eye and paste it on the side of a can, what do you have?" I waited a moment. "Why, of course — an 'eye can.' In fact," I explained, "an I CAN, spelled I C-A-N. Yesterday you couldn't tell me what an I CAN'T looked like, so I decided that today I would show you an I CAN."

All at once the idea clicked, and the change in attitudes was remarkable. No longer were they able to say, "I can't" in my classes. And you know, others enjoy being around those who are willing to say "I'll try."

Several weeks after I shared this philosophy at school, my Patti, who was only three years old then, said about something she had been asked to do, "Mama, I can't do that."

I said, "Oh, Patti, you mustn't say that word *can't;* I do not allow my students to say it, and I won't allow you to say it at home."

She looked at me and said, "Mama, I don't know how." At my house this is my philosophy: When you say *can't* it either means "I won't" or "I do not know how." If you do not know how, let me teach you; if you won't, then I'll spank you. I believe in giving everyone a choice, don't you?

My children are very familiar with my feelings about saying "I can't." I believe they've even come to share my feelings. Read Patti's poem below and see if you don't agree.

I CAN

I can, you see.
Everybody can,
even me.
Can't isn't a word.
It's dumb as a bird.
Look here and far.
Wherever you are.
There is no can't.
Not even an ant
can find can't.
So you see
it's up to me.
There's no such
word as
Can't.

2. *Diet.* The second most negative word in the English language is the word *diet.* There is no word that has been more used and abused in the last decade. It is negative because most of us just talk about going on a diet, but never actually do it. This is another case where positive doing is much more effective than talking. I heard a speaker say one time, "If we'd keep our mouths shut, we wouldn't be overweight." The truth hurts sometimes, doesn't it?

What the word actually means for us is <u>D</u>iscipline <u>I</u>n <u>E</u>ating <u>T</u>hings. Small adjustments can be made to our daily menu to avoid some of the unhealthy, high-cholesterol, fatty foods about which we are warned. Also, we need to be careful about being invited to someone's house or out to eat and letting our entire conversation be punctuated with "I shouldn't eat this, but —" as we eat our fourth homemade biscuit or dinner roll. If you are going to eat it, enjoy it and quit beating yourself over the head with that proverbial baseball bat. Decide your size and control it; quit boring others with your false expectations.

My sister Evelyn taught me something about size. She does not tell her size — she says she is fluffy. Several years ago she asked me if I would give her my hand-me-downs if she got down to my size ten. Surely, I would share them, I told her, and gave her one of my suits to demonstrate my faith that "if you can believe it, you can achieve it." I thought the positive imaging of her wearing the size ten suit would be reinforcement and encouragement for her.

She went back to Beaumont, and I did not hear from her for several months. I decided to call her one Saturday afternoon to chat. "By the way, Evelyn, how's the diet coming along?" There was a long pause at her end of the telephone. Finally, she said, "You know, Mamie, my bones are a size fourteen." She was actually saying that she was large and was planning to stay that way. She learned to accept her size and is a beautiful person.

3. *Nervous.* We are what we eat — we are what we say. We only need to look at ourselves to prove that we are what we eat. To prove that we are what we say, I'll tell you that I like to make fresh homemade lemonade. On a trip several years ago, I was given some beautiful California lemons. They were very large, bright yellow in color, and looked as if they were just right for lemonade. I picked them up, rolled them out on the kitchen counter and then took a knife and sliced them. As I was cutting through the lemons, so much juice poured out of them that it ran down all over the counter.

What is happening to your mouth? Uh-huh, is it watering? Right! You do not see a picture of a lemon on this page; however, your body is responding to it. In the same way, your body responds to words such as *nervous,* which means acute uneasiness. Your hands begin to perspire, your stomach may quiver, or your voice may shake. These reactions can be attributed to the fact that you have told yourself, "I am so nervous."

When you are in a stressful situation, it's not productive to tell yourself what you *don't* want; rather, tell yourself what you *do* want — to be calm, relaxed, and prepared. And sometimes we have to keep on telling ourselves.

Often, people are nervous about something because they aren't ready to perform their responsibilities. It is an insult to a group of people to admit, "I'm a little nervous, because I am not prepared." How many of us have wasted valuable time at meetings to have someone in charge admit, "I'm not prepared." *Bee* prepared and then say to yourself, *I am calm, I am relaxed, I am prepared.*

4. *Sick.* According to the American Medical Association, it is estimated that as many as 85 percent of the patients who go to the doctor do not need medical attention. This statistic makes a strong statement that being sick may possibly be an attitude and not a condition. Someone who says, "I'm sick and tired of this mess" really means "I'm bored and weary."

Maybe what we need, rather than a doctor, is a variation in what we are doing or an adjustment of our attitudes. Attitude does affect our bodies. Depression and poor self-image can cause physical aches and pains, so a positive attitude is remedial. If we talk about being sick, sick, sick, we talk ourselves into feeling bad. Avoid the word *sick.* Besides, other people do not want to hear about our ailments.

5. *Tired.* How many times have we said we are tired when actually we mean we are fatigued? Fatigued means a temporary feeling of low energy, both physical and emotional. *Tired* is the word to describe not being able to bounce back after a nap or a night's sleep. When we go to bed tired, get up tired, and remain tired all day, then we have a serious problem. Being fatigued is natural. We all have low times — my mama used to call them "the blues." We cannot succumb to this every time we feel a little down, though. Everyone is busy; everyone has more to do than he or she can get done. Don't bore your friends and family by telling them how tired you are. Hang in there. Endure. And remember Zig Ziglar's advice: "If we are tough on ourselves, then life will be easier on us."

SUCCESSFUL PEOPLE BATHE
MENTALLY EACH AND EVERY DAY

I took a bath yesterday and, lo and behold, I had to get up and take another bath today. We sleep each night, but we have to do that again — each night. Life demands that we repeat its processes. We must repeat some things in order to learn and grow and exist. Commitment to excellence requires this, too. Daily renewal is essential. Think of it as a mental bath, just as important as a hot soapy one. Refill your bucket so others can continue to dip from it; pray for the Lord to fill your cups. When we endeavor to do a task, the Lord will do 50 percent of it; but I've found He usually does the last 50 percent, testing to see if we have the willingness to start. Positive doing is not an inherited quality. We must learn it and practice, practice, practice each day — repeating it as automatically as we bathe or eat or sleep.

In addition to that, we must teach positive doing to others. We do this in three ways: example, example, example. But we teach in other ways as well. I have tried to set a good positive-doing example for my children, but I have instructed them along these lines, also. We started in simple ways when they were young, incorporating our beloved bumblebee idea into lists of positive-doing "do *bees*." Here is one of our first lists:

1. Do *bee* willing to read, read, read.

2. Do *bee* willing to speak to all you meet.

3. Do *bee* willing to memorize Heartitudes.

4. Do *bee* willing to listen to tapes, music, and speakers who motivate.

5. Do *bee* willing to have reminders or symbols of encouragement: a blue ribbon, an I CAN label, a bumblebee, an angel pin.

6. Do *bee* willing to associate with people who are smart and copy them.

Don't wait until it is too late with your children. Start on their education in positive doing when they are toddlers, learning the magic words of *please* and *thank you*. If they grow up in the I CAN philosophy, they will be positive doers all their lives. "Train up a child in the way he should go..." (Prov. 22:6).

Some of the best teaching is done with children's books. One of my favorites is a book by Judith Viorst, *Alexander and the Terrible, Horrible, No Good, Very Bad Day*. As the title indicates, Alexander's day began badly, continued to be bad and by the end of the day when he went to bed, he was disgusted with the world. He looked at everything and everybody as being against him, and he didn't want anything or anybody to change his mind. He was mad at the world. The book ends with Alexander saying to himself, *I think I'll just move to Australia.*

We have all had that feeling at times — wishing we could just get away from it all. It's okay to go to bed feeling down, but don't plan to get up feeling that way.

WHAT IS YOUR DECISION FOR TODAY?

I believe that we decide each night what kind of day we are going to have the next day. I also believe we are about as happy as we make up our minds to be. I heard that statement from my mama, and then I discovered that Abraham Lincoln is credited with saying it. Anyway, it is a truism that has been passed down, and one with which I strongly agree. People who make up their minds to be miserable are the kind of folks who seem to have had a "charisma bypass," as my good friend Thalia Hanna states. Remember, feelings follow actions. Proverbs says that when a person is gloomy, everything seems gloomy, but when he or she is cheerful, everything seems right.

If we base our day on how we feel when we get up each morning, then woe is me. I'm at the age when I put one foot out of the bed in the morning and the other foot says, "I ain't coming." However, I have found that after getting up and getting dressed, I begin to look better and to feel better. I have thought many times that the best work is done by those who do not start off "feeling like it." This has been proven to me often in my life.

One of my favorite and most often requested speeches is entitled "How to Be Up in a Down World." The focus of this speech is to encourage others to positive doing. Positive doing includes learning to communicate, something this story helps me illustrate:

There was a SCHOOL SUPERINTENDENT talking to his assistant superintendent. "Next Thursday at 10:30 a.m., Haley's Comet will appear over this area. This is an event which occurs only once every seventy-five years. Call the school principals and have them assemble their teachers and classes on their athletic fields and explain this phenomenon to them. If it rains, cancel the day's observations and have the classes meet in the auditorium to see a film about the comet."

Now, the ASSISTANT SUPERINTENDENT was to pass this on to the school principals. This is what the school principals heard: "By order of the superintendent of schools, next Thursday at 10:30, Haley's Comet will appear over your athletic field. If it rains, cancel the day's classes and report to the auditorium with your teachers and students, where you will be shown films, a phenomenal event which occurs once very seventy-five years.

The PRINCIPALS were asked to pass this on to the teachers. This is what the teachers heard: "By order of the phenomenal superintendent of schools, at 10:30 next Thursday, Haley's Comet will appear in the auditorium. In case of rain over the athletic field, the superintendent will give another order — something which occurs once every seventy-five years."

The TEACHERS were asked to pass this on to the students. This is what the students heard: "Next Thursday at 10:30, the superintendent of schools will appear in our school auditorium with Haley's Comet, something which occurs every seventy-five years. If it rains, the superintendent will cancel the comet and order us all out to our phenomenal athletic field."

The STUDENTS were asked to take this news home to their parents. This is what the parents heard: "When it rains next Thursday at 10:30 over the school athletic fields, the phenomenal seventy-five-year-old superintendent of schools will cancel all classes and appear before the whole school in the auditorium, accompanied by Bill Haley and the Comets."

A funny story, but it does prove a point. We must be able to communicate. Sue Davis, my teacher friend, tells her students, "I don't expect you to speak perfectly; but I do expect you to speak acceptably." If we want to maintain positive relationships with family, friends, and co-workers, we must not allow a breakdown in communication.

As I have already stated, positive doing requires daily commitment, daily practice, daily renewal. My attitude is my life. It's what I think and do all day long. Many years ago someone gave me this wonderful daily affirmation list. I have carried it in my billfold for years.

I promise myself...

To be so strong that nothing can disturb my peace of mind.

To talk health, happiness, and prosperity to every person I meet.

To make all my friends feel that there is something in them.

To look at the sunny side of everything and make my optimism come true.

To think only of the best, to work only for the best, and to expect only the best.

To be just as enthusiastic about the success of others as I am about my own.

To forget the mistakes of the past and press on to the greater achievements of the future.

To wear a cheerful countenance at all times and give every living creature I meet a smile.

To give so much time to the improvement of myself that I have no time to criticize others.

To be too large for worry, too noble for anger, too strong for fear, and too happy to permit the pressure of trouble.

In the above affirmation, notice the positive words: *optimism, sunny side, enthusiastic, cheerful countenance, smile, happy.* These are words that reflect the upbeat personality of a positive doer.

One of the easiest actions of a positive doer is to smile. When you are smiling, it is a physical impossibility to frown at the same time. I laughingly say that "a smile not given away will enlarge and settle in your hips." Now, that is fear motivation in its purest form! The following description of the effects of a smile appeared in an insurance advertisement. And I think it is worth sharing.

A smile costs nothing, but gives much. It enriches those who receive, without making poorer those who give. It takes a moment, but the memory of it sometimes lasts forever. None is so rich or mighty that he can get along without it, and none is so poor but that he can be made rich by it. A smile creates happiness in the home, fosters goodwill in business, and is the countersign of friendship. It brings rest to the weary, cheer to the discouraged, sunshine to the sad, and it is nature's best antidote for trouble. Yet it cannot be bought, begged, borrowed or stolen, for it is something that is of no value to anyone until it is given away. Some people are too tired to give you a smile. Give them one of yours, as no one needs a smile so much as he who has no more to give.

The next step after a smile is a laugh. There is nothing so friendly as a shared laugh. A laugh has to be good for the soul, and it is good for the body, as well.

Now, there is no evidence that laughter can cure the common cold, but statistics do show that regular doses of laughter may help to keep a person well, and it certainly relieves anxiety. "Laughter is a chemically stimulating experience. It stimulates the activity of most of the major physical systems of the human body," says Dr. William Fry of Stanford University. The average American laughs about fifteen times a day, ranging from a giggle to a belly laugh. Some especially jolly people may laugh as many as one hundred or more times a day. So along with our smiles, let's laugh a little too. It's an internal job. Be willing to laugh at yourself and be able to take a joke. And when you laugh, make sure you are laughing *with* people, not *at* them.

PUT WD-40 ON YOUR DREAM MACHINE

When we dream, are we engaging in positive doing? Of course we are, if we have a plan to go along with those dreams. Henry Thoreau said, "If you build castles in the air, that's where they should be. Now, put foundations under them." *That* is positive doing.

I get letters from so many people that say, "I've lost all hope. I have nothing to dream for." One of the reasons that we get so discouraged is that we either do not have a dream or we lose it. I think one of the ways that we can stay motivated and positive is to keep remembering how to dream. One of the purposes of this book is to put some WD-40 on your dream machine.

In some of my seminars, I ask people to pretend. I call it "play-like." Play-like you are only eight years old. It's a warm, summer day. You and your best friend are swinging on your grandmother's front porch. The smell of gingerbread is coming out of the window. As you sit there with anticipation of the gingerbread and playing with your best friend, you say, "What are we going to do when we grow up?"

Can you take yourself back to when you were eight and forget about what you know now, what your circumstances are? Just play-like for a minute. What are some of the dreams that you might have had when you were eight, ten, twelve, sixteen, twenty, or thirty years old?

Some of the most exciting people I know are people who still have dreams. In fact, one of them is a new friend of mine, Irene Dankly, from Coral Gables, Florida. I met her while speaking at a seminar in California. She called recently and said she couldn't talk to me long that night because she was on her way to a computer class.

I said, "Irene, you're eighty years old." I thought I had misunderstood or had a bad connection.

"No," she said, "you didn't misunderstand. My grandchildren are learning the computer, and I have to keep up! I had to take the course, too."

We cannot avoid getting older, but we can certainly avoid getting old. I think having goals and dreams is one of the ways that we can keep from getting old. We need dreams.

I have a couple of dreams that I would like to share with you. One is that I would like to have a home. All I know about the home is that it is a two-story house with ten bedrooms and a porch that goes all the way around it. This house sits among some trees near a lake or stream, something to do with water. I have a specific picture of this home in my mind, and I dream of calling it something like "A Dose of Hope," "A Hopeful House," or "Where People Can Come To Rest."

Looking back on some of the periods in my life, I made some wrong decisions, and I feel that I made those wrong decisions because I was tired. Like many of you, I worked hard most of my life, and I never took time out to rest when I needed to make good decisions. As I said earlier, I believe that a lot of times mistakes could be avoided if we could just make the decisions with a rested mind.

My dream is to have this home where troubled, tired people can come for five days to recuperate. There will be a homemade quilt on every bed — no television, no telephones. There will be a garden and a swing on the porch where guests can go to pray or meditate or just rest and rethink their lives.

Yes, it is a dream. However, I realize why a lot of dreams do not come true: carelessness, laziness, temptation, and unconcern. I believe in putting legs on dreams, and I have *started*.

Dare to dream; get excited!

On my fiftieth birthday, my friend Margie Wynn asked me what my favorite Bible verse was, and I told her Jeremiah 33:3, "Call unto me, and I will answer thee, and show thee great and mighty things, which thou knowest not." She said, "Mamie, I would like to do a painting for you with that scripture."

I had never spoken to Margie — or anyone — about my dream of the home. When I received the picture, I sat down and cried because as I looked at the picture, I knew that it was the picture of the home that I someday wanted to share with others. How could Margie possibly have created a painting that so exactly captured my vision of this dream home? The watercolor shows blue skies and green pastures surrounding a beautiful white two-story structure. The house is large (to accommodate those who need such a refuge), but it has the intimate appearance of a cozy cottage. It has a blue roof and blue shutters. The large porch includes a swing. And, yes, beside the house is a placid lake. God showed Margie my house!

Today, when I pass that picture in my living room, it gives me a dose of hope because it's a reminder of one of my dreams.

Another of my dreams is to have a place in my yard where people can come to meditate. I have in mind a prayer chapel, a small building with natural light where people can come and sit down and reflect.

When I was in a church in California about ten years ago, I saw a beautiful picture of Jesus' hands; in fact, I bought the print. It's in my home now. So, in my dream, I have a small chapel with a stained-glass window picturing those outreached hands which say to everyone who sees them, "Come unto Me with your burdens and cares, and I will help you."

I feel that no room is complete without an angel. I have an angel in every room of my house. My mental picture of the little chapel has some guardian angels around it. When and how my goal of building that chapel will be reached, I do not know; but when I get discouraged, physically or mentally fatigued, I think about some of my dreams and this keeps me going.

Until that dream home becomes a reality, you may write to me anytime for a complimentary copy of my newsletter, *The Encourager*, at the following address:

Mamie McCullough
305 Spring Creek Village
Dallas, TX 75248
(972) 437-5308 or
(800) 255-4226

SOMEONE IS ALWAYS WATCHING

I'm sure we've all had the experience of working past the time when we were charming. One hot, humid July day in 1987 was that kind of day for me. I had been traveling for a couple of weeks, so you can imagine not only how tired I was but how far behind I was with correspondence. For about ten hours I dictated correspondence, returned calls, edited I CAN materials, and attended two meetings. To say the least, I did not feel — and neither did I look — charming.

When I left my office, I had no intention of seeing anyone, so why bother with combing my hair or freshening up my makeup? After all, no one that I new would see me. A million people live in Dallas; chances were excellent that I would not see anyone I knew.

I was about six blocks from home when I remembered that I needed to stop by the Baptist Book Store to pick up some books for a women's prayer group which I was starting at the office the next morning. I pulled into a parking space, started to look in the mirror, but thought, *No one knows you in this store. Don't bother with your appearance.* "Dog tired," I slowly walked into the store, asked for the materials, and waited while the clerk graciously went to get the books. I began looking around the store and noticed a large display of books by new authors, but mine was not there. *I CAN. You Can TOO!* had been out only a couple of weeks, but I had been told by my publisher that the Baptist Book Stores were carrying my book and my book was not there.

Have you ever been so tired that you wanted to pick a fight with someone — just anyone? *Well,* I thought, *you would think that since I'm Baptist, surely they should support my efforts.* I seethed.

The clerk graciously took my money, gave me the materials, and thanked me. I decided to ask her about the book but not tell her who I was. I said, "By the way, I understand there is a new book out called *I Can. You Can Too!* and I thought perhaps you all would have it." I expected an excuse for why they did not have it.

However, she replied, "Oh, yes, we do carry it. We do not know the author personally, but we understand she lives here in Dallas. We bought only a case of the books, and they sold quickly. We are presently out, but are keeping a list of people who want it —" (she pushed a long yellow pad at me). "If you will write your name and telephone number, we will call you the minute the books arrive."

There I stood looking at a list of people who wanted my new book. I was a little taken aback but decided this was too good to let pass so I replied, "I am Mamie McCullough." She smiled, gave me a big hug, and asked for my autograph. I left that store with my head high, feeling like a million dollars. As my mama would say, "I pressed out." Just five minutes before, I had felt like I was down under. Then, without eating a meal, swallowing a vitamin pill, or taking a nap, I was suddenly renewed and refreshed. The difference was in my attitude. Many times we need to evaluate our situation and give ourselves a mental checkup. If we are down, maybe it's our attitude that needs changing.

When we identify what we need to do, let's "just do it," and we'll always be glad we did. Positive thinking is important. But it's just one part of a more important step — positive doing.

GET IT TOGETHER — HERE'S HOW:

1. Put gratitude in your attitude. Be grateful for what you have, giving thanks at all times.

2. Make the I CAN way of life your way of life.

3. Eliminate negative words such as: *can't, diet, nervous, sick, tired.* We are what we eat. We are what we say. Here are suggestions for replacement words

I can't	I'll try
D.I.E.T.	Good nutrition
Nervous	I'm calm. I'm relaxed. I'm prepared.
Sick and tired	Well and happy

4. Follow the example of people who bathe each day, mentally. We have to bathe our bodies each day in order to stay clean and healthy. So we must bathe our minds also with daily doses of good books, tapes, and friends.

5. Construct your own Do *Bee* list. Encourage all family members to help set up rules for your home. After all, we have rules for school, church, the IRS — why not home? ASK in order to GET.

6. Practice good manners. They will always be popular and appreciated.

7. Smile. To receive a smile brightens the day for anyone — including the one who gives it. A smile is the same in any language.

CHAPTER 8

How Many Happy Selfish People Do You Know?

Even though I receive hundreds of letters from people who have terrible problems, and although I speak to thousands who are hurting, I still encounter many happy, contented people. They might be rich or poor, old or young, white or black. There seems to be only one common denominator among happy people: I have never seen a selfish person who was happy. Contentedness and selfishness just don't go together — they do not mix.

True, we live in a society that has become the "I-me-my" age. First person singular. "Listen to me," "me first," "do it my way," "I want," "it's not my fault," "what about me?" "I'm number one." Aren't you sick to death of hearing from people who are concerned only for themselves?

We parents may be partly to blame. We indulge our children because we want them to have things we did not have, or we are too busy to train them to be capable adults. We teach our children to be selfish and grasping, to get to the top at all costs, trampling those in the way. We cannot live that way!

♥ • ♥ • ♥ • ♥ • ♥

HEARTITUDE

Give the Gift That Lives On: Yourself

♥ • ♥ • ♥ • ♥ • ♥

Do not misunderstand, there are many unselfish people out there, but they are the quiet ones — the ones we don't hear. We must turn things around; we must cultivate loving, caring people. The good news is that some evidence indicates this general trend may be occurring right now.

I believe a key word in this problem is *consideration*. We have not taught this generation to be considerate of others' feelings. We are not careful about "doing unto others as we would have them do unto us."

On September 16, 1989, *USA Today* had a headline which read: "A Gift for Those Who'd Rather Give Than Get." It stated that, according to Jim Dureger, Public Support Vice President of the American Red Cross, during 1989 people seemed to be giving to charitable organizations, rather than giving the traditional gifts to each other. The article also quoted Ruth Brinker, Founder and Executive Officer of Project Open Hand, which provides meals for AIDS patients. "The 'Me First Era' is past," she said.

I believe giving is contagious. We do not all have the expertise to help the at-risk students, the ones on drugs, the AIDS victims, the college students, the poor, or many of the nonprofit organizations. However, there is one mutual gift that all of these people and groups need: our money and our prayers. The gift is never too small or too large — my experience is that it is always appreciated. To volunteer with one of these organizations, to become perhaps a partner in education, to speak to a group of volunteers, or to write a note of appreciation for what they're doing can add to their hopes and dreams. Perhaps doing something special for the staff members can be an encouragement for them. Sometimes their buckets get empty and need refilling. Just because these workers are in a giving environment does not mean they do not also have needs.

It is never too late to develop into a caring person, if you truly want to overcome selfishness. Learning how to care is a lifelong process.

What can we do to teach people to be tender, kind, caring, unselfish individuals? Take small steps. Begin by consciously performing considerate acts for those around you, thereby teaching by example. For some people who are not naturally unselfish, this takes conscious effort and constant practice. Think of others first. Listen to and remember the joys and sorrows of those around you, and then make an honest effort to show love and interest in those concerns.

Do you remember the story of Ebenezer Scrooge in Charles Dickens' *Christmas Carol*? He was a selfish, mean, unhappy old man, concerned only with making money and pleasing himself. As the story progressed, he realized his shortcomings and made a complete turnaround. At last, his concern was for others, and he gave rather than took; he shared rather than stored; he thought of ways to help others. Overnight he became the happiest man in town, because he became concerned for others. He laughed; he smiled; he danced in the streets, because he was freed from his self-centeredness.

If only we could show the selfish people in this world the joy of giving! As Ben Sweetland stated, "We cannot hold a torch to light another's path without brightening our own."

The world acclaims many generous, giving people who have dedicated their lives to others. One of the most notable of these is Mother Teresa, a woman who has been an inspiration to all of us because of her caring spirit. Some caregivers are ordinary citizens who have a full-time job seeing after handicapped children, infants, or elderly relatives.

There is a current generation that is unique in that they are simultaneously caring for their young adult children, as well as their elderly parents. These people are the unsung heroes and heroines of our day. Their contribution to our society cannot be estimated, but their love and concern are evident.

Ruth and Bill Singleton live in Detroit, and their love story began fifty-one years ago. Handsome, young, and industrious, the couple eloped, because her parents would not approve the marriage. Bill had two jobs at two different automobile plants to provide for his family. The primary job of the Singletons was nurturing their family. Starting with little, they created a good life using hard work, willpower, and love. They managed to rear fifteen children who claim that they never felt poor or neglected. The amazing part of the story is that the couple also raised a grandson from birth, along with a nephew.

How did they do it? With an unselfish lifetime of love, care, and generosity. "Work is love made visible," Ruth says, "and God never gives you a higher mountain than you can climb."

In this day and time when we have so much pampered affluence, we often are at a loss as to what to give loved ones and friends on special occasions such as birthdays, anniversaries, and Christmas. Many times we need to give more than something with a price tag bought at a store; we need to give of ourselves. David Dunn has written a book entitled *Try Giving Yourself Away* in which he reminds us that the gift of self is the most precious and sought-after gift. It is the gift of great value which has no price tag; it cannot be lost or forgotten; it comes in one size that fits all; it is the gift that really keeps on giving. It is the gift of *yourself*. This is the essence of unselfishness, a true gift from heart to heart, which is always given in love and received as such. No one has ever been offended by a love gift.

When I was growing up "poor" in rural South Georgia, I had no choice — I had no money, so I had to learn to be creative. Giving homemade corsages was one of my favorite things to do for my Sunday school teacher, Miss Bowen. On Sunday morning, I would get up early to pick the beautiful dew-dripped running roses from the fence along the dusty country road. Then when the beautiful lilies would bloom, I would use some of them to make an original, intricate, personalized corsage just for Miss Bowen. (I would always have to rush to church before the flowers wilted.) As I look back, I realize how crudely the gift was made. I would have only sewing thread to keep it together and a big safety pin to pin it on. But when I would take those flowers to her, she would smile and give me a big hug, always kissing me on the top of the head. I will never forget her love and kindness toward me.

Although I'm sure the corsages were not attractive, I believe she knew they came from my heart and were all I had to give, and she always treated my gesture with kindness. She was the church pianist, and I'll always remember how proud I was to see her sitting on that piano bench, displaying my often wilted gift of flowers.

(In those days I never realized that I would ever be able to keep fresh flowers in my house as I do today. That is one of the "little joys" I have in going to the grocery store — to come back home with fresh flowers, even in winter.)

The kindness shown to me by Miss Bowen has encouraged me to use my creativity in many other ways, and I encourage you to pass this concern along to the young.

When my mother passed away in 1978, we went through her keepsakes, and there, in the bottom of the old musty-smelling trunk, we found some of my grade school "originals." She had neatly placed in a stack the paper-plate wall hangings with flowers cut out of the *Progressive Farmer.* I remember with joy those days when she would hang them in her kitchen.

Things given of the heart are the only ones with lasting power. *Gifts of the heart touch the heart.* Try giving yourself away. There is no end to this reservoir.

It is overwhelming to me at times to realize how much of ourselves is passed down through our children. Because my mother and family encouraged me, I have felt the freedom to encourage my children to be creative and unselfish by giving the best gift of all — unselfish love.

WE SOW WHAT WE REAP

When my children's father died in 1981, I realized how financially strapped we were going to be for a while. It was ridiculous to give the kids money to buy me cards or gifts for special occasions, so I told them that from then on, they would have to make my cards or gifts if they wanted me to have something. I found that this practice encouraged their creativity, as well as helped with the family budget. At first, it was short verses, which moved into stories, all of which I have kept in a box marked "Children's Treasures."

Christmas

Christmas, is fun and joys,
It's when you get lots of toys.

Christmas is decorating a tree,
It's as fun as it can be.

Christmas, when family comes,
That's when it's so much fun.

Christmas, is when you sit
around a fire so warm.

But most of all it was when
Jesus was born.

Merry Chistmas

Patti M'Collough, age 10

A very important part of raising unselfish people is teaching them to give something which they create. "The Fust Christmas" was one of Jennifer's first writings when she was in the second grade.

THE FUST CHRISTMAS

by Jennifer Mc.

Onece a pon there was a long time ago win a baby was fixing to be born and the Parins had know war to have him isapt outside so some one said I am to croded in my house any way so you can stay in my cow barn and they spinded the night there and they had a babyt and all the shapers and pepple came to see the baby and the angle said he must be named preshus lord jesus and ruler of the world and than I can rember a lot of Rules. Do not still Mind your father and mother

The End

You can readily see that this is from her heart and is her understanding of the Christmas story.

At age ten, Patti wrote the Christmas poem on the preceding page; however, she actually told what Christmas meant to her with the accompanying illustrations.

Each of these writings is unique, but both show the gift of true giving. What they've given me is joy. How happy each of these has made me and others with whom I have shared them during the years!

WE HELP OURSELVES AS WE HELP OTHERS

I am forever trying to give you readers some short strategies, little hints, and small steps to help you *bee* better. Here are some to help you *bee* happy by being unselfish.

Give a hug for affirmation to someone.

Give a note of encouragement.

Give a deed of kindness — open a door, smile, speak.

Give a visit to a lonely person.

Give an hour of your time to listen.

Give a phone call to someone for no reason — just call.

Give a flower.

Give a Sunday dinner.

Just make it a way of life to give. A part of yourself is the most important gift; it shows your unselfishness and always makes others happy. Passing on a part of ourselves truly does make us "agents of God," and in the process we become better people.

I have had people tell me that although they want to give, they feel embarrassed at trying to do something for others. I understand this, but just the same, I would encourage you to *start*. Try — I mean make an intentional effort to reach out to others. Remember, everyone we meet is hurting in some way. If you are shy, practice speaking a word of kindness or encouragement to just one extra person a day. Practice, practice, practice until you are comfortable in speaking. *Give the gift that lives on: yourself.*

I am convinced that when we encourage others, we improve ourselves: we get a lift, we feel good inside, and we take a step toward achieving peace and contentment. Functioning unselfishly makes us happy. Therefore, encouraging others is one of those positive actions we can take to *bee* better ourselves. It costs nothing and it reaps such great benefits to encourage someone who is depressed with life or who is discouraged with a job or a marriage. We are all hurting in some way, and encouragement is a real boost when we are down.

The educators of Texas are convinced that encouragement is a method that all teachers should use, so much so that they have a complete section on encouragement in the current appraisal document. Teachers are graded by their supervisors on their encouragement skills. And what are some of these skills?

1. Make it clear that you care for the person you wish to encourage.

2. Say "I love you" often.

3. Use words such as *good, great, fantastic, good job, well done, that's right, right on,* or *super.*

4. Hug or touch a hand or a shoulder.

5. Give the "thumbs up" sign to remind the person that he or she is "thumbbody."

6. Smile and call people by their names.

7. Leave notes of encouragement.

8. Praise.

9. Give rewards — a blue ribbon or a sticker.

10. Listen to problems and provide a shoulder to cry on when necessary.

These are just a few actions that we can take to show others we are interested in them. Because these actions help us lose our self-centeredness, we also help ourselves as we help others.

I read a wonderful story about a boy named Teddy in Tony Campolo's *Who Switched the Price Tags?* Teddy Stallard was one of those negative students who sits at the back of the room with a chip on his shoulder — disinterested, disruptive, and not very clean. He was not lovable, not cooperative, not a favorite of Ms. Thompson, his teacher. He barely complied with the dress code.

At Christmas all the students, including Teddy, brought Ms. Thompson gifts. When she opened Teddy's gift, she discovered cheap perfume and an old bracelet of his mother's. She dabbed on some of the perfume and put on the bracelet, telling Teddy how pleased she was. It was a giant effort for Ms. Thompson to pretend such pleasure, but it made Teddy look good in front of his peers.

This was a turning point for Teddy and for Ms. Thompson. She started encouraging Teddy in many ways and he responded. In turn, Ms. Thompson became a better, more understanding teacher, not only to Teddy but to all the students.

As time went on, Teddy graduated with honors and eventually became a doctor. When he married, he asked Ms. Thompson to represent his family at the wedding because by now both his parents were dead.

To me, this is a real success story, a real win-win. Through persistent effort, Ms. Thompson encouraged Teddy to do something with his life, and his accomplishments brought happiness, contentment, and pride to her.

THOSE WHO AFFECT THE LIFE OF A CHILD AFFECT GENERATIONS TO COME

Encouragement pays off in the business world as well as in our schools. For fifteen years I was the manager of a company, so I know the problems of the corporate structure. Also, more and more, I am addressing people in the world of business — executives, managers, owners, and high-level employees, as well as members of the sales force.

I think all companies — large or small — must have a heart. Some companies are under so much pressure from their stockholders to make bigger and bigger profits that they forget about their employees. Top-level executives encourage their people to be family, church, and community oriented, but too often they do that to make the company look good, not to make the employees feel important or cared for. Caring companies build self-esteem in their people who, as a result, show a happiness and an *esprit de corps* that calloused, uncaring companies do not have.

At a recent seminar, I asked a group of top-level executives how they encouraged their employees, and they were hard pressed to answer. They looked as though it had never occurred to them to encourage their workers. After all, they paid them a salary! Finally, one of the managers said that he occasionally thanked an employee. But it didn't take these intelligent men long to get the idea. Pretty soon, they were having the time of their lives thinking of all kinds of ways to encourage.

I always tell top-level management that one of my goals is to make them look good after I leave. If they improve their company relationships,

I have done that. Companies, like individuals, must have a heart. When they do, business improves as people improve.

I am so convinced that *encouragement* is a magic word, that my quarterly newsletter is entitled *The Encourager.* My mission in life is to encourage those who have problems, and that is everybody. Don't think it is you by yourself if sometimes you feel depressed, rejected, and isolated. I understand. I have been there, and I know the value of encouragement.

George Bernard Shaw said in *Pygmalion:* "The difference between being a lady and not being one lies in how she is treated." As we treat others, so in time they will become.

GET IT TOGETHER — HERE'S HOW:

1. Be involved in lifting others up if you wish to be truly happy.

2. Try being creative in helping others. Small gifts of yourself are wonderful presents. Giving is contagious.

3. Pattern your life after people who have built others up with love, kindness, and encouragement.

4. Practice the art of hugging, touching, and reaching out in creative ways. This could be a pat on a child's head, a flower, a card, a telephone call, or a genuine hug. I believe hugs are a necessary part of life. I say, if it moves, feed it and hug it; if it doesn't, dust it or sell it! The point is to acknowledge those around you.

5. Tell people you genuinely love and appreciate them. Write notes of encouragement.

CHAPTER 9

OVERCOMING REJECTION

If Winter comes, can Spring be far behind?
—*Percy Bysshe Shelley*

Unfortunately, the world is full of rejection stories. Have you heard the one about —

Little Jenni? She is in kindergarten — a sweet, sincere little five-year-old, the apple of her father's eye. The kids were playing "Red Rover, Red Rover, will you come over?" Jenni wanted desperately to play. But she was not chosen.

Tyler? He is in the seventh grade — pretty good student but crazy to play football. He practiced and did everything the coach demanded. And then he sat on the bench.

Mike? He is a graduating senior — popular, good-looking, likable. He planned to attend college to become an engineer. But the university refused his application.

Cindy? High school graduate — cute, irresponsible, affectionate. She wanted to marry and have a baby. Her high school sweetheart married her best friend.

Carter? Graduate of a good law school — intelligent, sincere, industrious. He wanted a job with a good law firm. But the companies were not hiring.

♥ • ♥ • ♥ • ♥ • ♥

HEARTITUDE

Turn Your Scars Into Stars

♥ • ♥ • ♥ • ♥ • ♥

Leslie? Housewife and mother — gracious, attractive, devoted. She wanted to maintain a stable home for the family. Then she found out her husband was having an affair with his secretary.

William and Katherine? Parents of a teenager — unselfish, frugal, kind. They wanted nothing but the best for their children. Now their son was in a drug rehabilitation center.

Do these stories sound familiar? Can you personally identify with any of them? Do you know Jenni? Tyler? Mike? Cindy? Carter? Leslie? The answer almost surely has to be yes, because these stories are all too common. Or perhaps we see ourselves in one of these examples. We have all experienced rejection in life — maybe many times. Some of us have been rejected so often that we have come to perceive ourselves as losers.

Rejection is so hurtful. We feel crushed that we are not wanted. We start wondering, *"What is the matter with me, anyway?"* It is important that we process these hurts and deal with them positively. How many times have I mentioned in this book already that we all hurt in some way, at some time? It is universal and we must face the problem and defeat it.

"You hurt my feelings." Hurt, hurt, hurt. What a cruel world. When you remember a hurtful situation, does your body actually flinch with the memory? Do you become nauseous? Can you feel the pain? Yes, yes, yes. I know. I understand. When you are deeply hurt, you cannot calm the inner fears and agonies. No one seems to understand the battle you are going through. The pain is real. The hurt becomes physical, but there is no physical cure. There is, however, a circle of healing, as described here and depicted in the diagram on the next page.

We hurt: Many times in our lives we have things which are intentionally and unintentionally done to us that hurt. In this decade hurt is so evident in newspaper articles and items on the nightly news describing people hurting themselves and hurting each other. The high level of suicide among people of all ages indicates to us just how much some people do hurt. Once we are hurt, we can only take the facts and process them until they are not so hurtful to us. We will always have the scars of hurt, but the hurt can be lessened by processing.

HURT–HEAL CYCLE

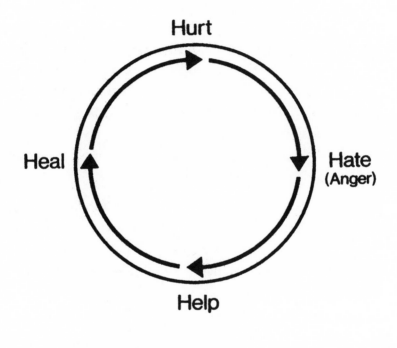

We hurt
We hate
We get help
We begin to heal

We hate (feel anger): Whether it is something someone has said to us, neglect, or a form of abuse — verbal, emotional, physical, or sexual — we do feel anger when we are hurt. If turned inward and not outward, or if it's not processed, the anger will cause many, many problems, both now and also later in life. It is natural to have anger, but do not let it stop the cycle of hurt or anger. Anger turned inward causes depression.

We get help: Help may be obtained from others such as family members, friends, counselors, our church, or other professionals. We can receive help from reading the Bible and other books which give us hope. Cassette and video tapes are very accessible; even libraries have sections from which they can be checked out. Remember, it is the input that determines our output. We need to be constantly putting in the positive to outweigh the negative. We never take one dose of anything that lasts a lifetime; never can hurt be processed that easily, even when an apology is made. Please, please get the kind of help that you need. Do not allow the negatives of the world to eat you up.

We heal: All healing takes time. When we admit that we hurt, then healing begins. It takes a lot of input on a daily basis to keep the old sore from being sensitive. My experience is that even old scars seem to be less conspicuous and are hardly noticeable after time and help. Keep the cycle going. Turn your scars into stars.

We hurt, we are angry, we get help, and then we heal. It is a cycle that needs to be addressed as a fact of life. When we get hungry, we eat; when we hurt, we heal. Make that process a way of life.

In our analysis of the problem of rejection, we have addressed the act of rejection itself, the resulting hurt that accompanies the act, and the necessary circle of healing. Now we must assert, "Yes, I have been rejected; yes, I have been hurt. But I am not worthless, and I am not a "throw back." But we do need some specific positive-doing suggestions that will enable us to deal with our rejection. Determine to put the following actions into your life. Work hard at it daily.

1. *Talk it out.* Talk the rejection over with close family or friends. It will help to bring it all out into the open. Please remember to be honest

in relating what your feelings are and discuss them with one who will not blame, tell, or make you feel guilty. And be careful to tell only those who can help you solve the problem.

2. *Learn to laugh.* Laughing actually will cause your mind and body to relax and you will be able to think more rationally. Learn to look at the situation knowing that *failure is an event, not a person.*

3. *Be physical.* Get rid of excess stress, depression, hate, and resentment by exercising. Twenty minutes of fast walking four times a week will do wonders for your attitude.

4. *Be emotional.* Cry if you need to; get your anger out where you can process it. Scream and stomp your feet if it helps. Throw a "pity party," but put a time limit on it.

5. *Remember: there have been some good times.* Also remember: it will not always be like this. All things change. We have to look at where we've been and decide not to make that mistake or error again.

6. *Understand: we have all fallen down.*

7. *Recognize: it is not easy to forgive and forget.* This is a process that should be taken seriously. Remember the cycle of hurt that we must continue to process: hurt, hate (anger), receive help, and continue to heal.

8. *Associate with people who love, care, and understand your hurt.* They prop us up.

One other small step that I might mention while this healing process is going on is to keep smiling. The world loves a lover. After all, we are I CAN people (I CAN being a way of life), and we need to look the part. I don't mean for you to suppress your hurt and anger, but don't turn into a solemn martyr either. You mustn't wallow in self-pity. When you are smiling, it is hard to hold a grudge. And our faces often tell the whole story.

One hot summer evening, I was in the kitchen preparing dinner (this was before I learned to tell the children to go get in the car when they got hungry). We were all hot and tired, the phone kept ringing, the doorbell was forever chiming, and the kids were noisy — it was not a pleasant time.

Then Brian came into the kitchen and said, "Mama, why are you mad?"

"I'm not mad, Brian, take out the garbage," I said as I continued to cook.

He took out the garbage and came back in. "Mama, why are you mad?"

"Brian, I'm not mad — set the table."

He set the table; then..."Mama, why are you mad?"

I had had it! I turned to him, looked down into his amazed face and said, "Brian, why do you think I'm mad? I am just busy getting dinner ready. What makes you think I'm mad?"

He looked up at me very seriously and said, "Well, if you're not mad, you surely should notify your face."

So many times, we give off the wrong signals. Because of preoccupation with getting things together, we miscommunicate. We need to stop and evaluate what message we are sending out to others. Many times we look mad when, in essence, we are busy.

GET IT TOGETHER — HERE'S HOW:

1. We all experience rejection; accept it and try not to go down that road again.

2. Feelings follow action. Start moving and you'll feel and respond better.

3. We hurt, hate, get help, and heal. Keep the cycle of hurt moving. Rejection becomes easier to accept once we begin the healing cycle.

4. Turn your scars into stars. I believe we are not accountable for what happens to us, but for what we make out of the situation. When we help others through their hurt, we turn scars into stars.

CHAPTER 10

YOU CAN COME BACK FROM DEFEAT

The world breaks everyone and afterward many are strong at the broken place.

—*Ernest Hemingway*

To be *defeated* or to be *successful* — those conditions have exactly opposite meanings. Everyone fails sooner or later. Failure is a normal part of life. It is something all of us need to learn how to handle so that when we are defeated we can deal with the situation and pull ourselves back up. Success and defeat are both processes — neither happens overnight. If we do not deal with failure properly, we will only get bitter and fail again. Human nature is such that, when we fail at something, we must learn to look at the event as a temporary situation and not take it as a permanent condition. Remember, *failure is an event, not a person.*

The Bible has many examples of human failure. *Defeat and depression* are not new words — they have been around a long time and will continue to be with us. Abraham was guilty of lying, adultery, and laughing at God, yet is remembered as the father of the faithful. Samson fell to Delilah, yet was Israel's greatest warrior. God can still use us if we don't give up and quit. *Never quit!*

To come back from defeat, we must first understand it as a universal part of being human and then accept responsibility for the outcome of

♥•♥•♥•♥•♥

HEARTITUDE

True Success Is Not Avoiding Failure, But Learning What To Do With It

♥•♥•♥•♥•♥

our actions. We must learn from our failures. We especially need to learn how not to make the same mistakes again and again. We all have weaknesses, so whatever can be changed, let's change. Whatever needs to be improved, let's improve. None of us has the talents and abilities to succeed at everything. We all have areas in which our talents and abilities are limited. We know at what and how we best function, so we should not try to be something that we're not. We cannot all be ballplayers, singers, or corporate executives — but some of us can speak and encourage, and when we feel that is our "mission," we should *do* it!

I have counseled with people who have spent their entire lives feeling like failures because they could not succeed at everything they wanted to do. Sometimes when we have initial defeats early on, we get discouraged and angry, and then never seem to accomplish what we could have done had we kept on trying.

My good friend Rena Tarbet, National Sales Director of Mary Kay Cosmetics, has fought cancer for over ten years. She is a beautiful, successful, talented businesswoman who has much to give to others. When she first discovered she had cancer she said, "I want God to use me, sick or well." We must believe that God will be with us "through thick and thin" and trust His promise to us that He will not leave us comfortless. Remember, though, He did not say He would leave us comfortable.

When people fail, they usually do one of two things — either they confess their failure, repent of it, and get right with God and humankind, or they go around making excuses for the failure. The first group gets back on track, and ultimately they turn their failures into successes. The latter group never honestly faces the failures. They never solve the problems that led to those failures and their lives never get turned around. When we do the right thing, we are forgiven and our failures are erased in God's sight.

As I look back over my life of more than fifty years, I see many hills and many valleys. Some were short, flat hills, and some of the valleys were deep and rough for a long period of time. Someone once said, "The best fruit grows in the valleys, not on the mountaintop." As with our lives, we grow and learn in the valleys of defeat and despair. The first time I suffered from depression, I would never admit that it really was depression, because I felt weak and embarrassed. I thought of it as an "unmentionable" ailment. Therefore, it was difficult to get help because I would not talk about it or seek advice. If an airplane pilot doesn't know how to use instruments when he flies through clouds or storms, he will not be able to stay on course because he doesn't have the horizon on which to focus. If he tries to adjust the instrument without proper knowledge, even a small adjustment might mean catastrophe.

People who get into deep depression and guilt are often like the pilot without instructions. What they need is outside help to give them some direction and help them regain their equilibrium. Otherwise they can get into a tailspin, with devastating results.

Other helpers may offer just small adjustments, but sometimes that's all we need to get back on course where we can see the horizon again. We are made so that we need to seek guidance and direction — instructions — from other people. For some people, this is a very difficult thing to do; nevertheless, it is a necessary step in processing our feelings.

When I was a child, I thought if I ever got to be twenty years old and could have a big-brimmed Sunday hat, then all my frustrations, problems, and hurts would be gone. Not so. Hopefully, however, most of us do live and learn from our experiences.

A book I saw on a display table at a local store had an intriguing title: *Bumps Are What We Climb On.* How true this is to life. Without bumps we would all be "wimps." I remember Mama saying, "Hard times build character." There have been times in my life when I had to say, "Oh, Lord, please don't build my character anymore today." I thought I had all the character I needed. But think again. Life is a building process and when we are "torn down" by events and people in our life, we must build ourselves back up and go on.

What we want out of life is basically unrealistic. We want to stay within the norm and not always "peak out" on the highs or "bottom out" on the lows, as shown in the accompanying graph. It would be nice to have life in such order that when we get one thing in our life straightened out, everything else would stay straight. Our lives run on the same pattern as my house: I cook, we eat, I cook, we eat. We have to cook for each meal and we have to handle life's failures the same way.

Highs in life

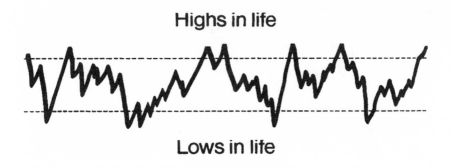

Lows in life

FAILURE OR DEFEAT

1. To fail is normal and human. We all fail. We all fall short and we all have limitations. True success is not avoiding failure, but learning what to do with it.

2. Failure is an event, not a person. Studies show that the most successful people often fail. We all strike out in life, but keep on batting just like Babe Ruth. Look at Lee Iacocca — he was fired from Ford only to come back and put Chrysler on the map. The history books are full of successful failures. The only way not to drown is to keep coming back up for one more bit of air.

3. We are not failures or defeated until we stop trying. But some people are actually scared of trying. They never accomplish anything because they have the fear of failing. It is better to attempt much and occasionally fail than to attempt nothing and achieve it. No one learns the limits of his ability until he has reached the point of total failure. Had Thomas Edison quit the first time he "failed," we would perhaps not have the modern electric light. I would never label Mr. Edison as a failure;

however, he did fail five thousand times in experimenting with different types of light-bulb filaments before he found the one that worked.

Success is failure with the dirt brushed off. We try; we get dirty; we get up, brush ourselves off, and try again. Do not ever quit trying. Not trying is sure defeat.

Success always consists of small, simple steps or small, "bite-size" components. The computer has zillions of small, simple components which make it possible to print, paint, draw, and perform many other functions (which I have not mastered to date).

When we realize our capabilities and use them, we grow, learn, and overcome. My computer is useless to me until I turn it on and begin to type and — yes, make mistakes, which if corrected soon enough, will ultimately become pages for this book.

Implement a plan of action which is best for you. We sometimes want to have others make it easy for us to overcome a mistake or come back from failure, but this is a "do it yourself" job. A plan, perhaps, will be trial and error. It will involve developing *persistence* above all else. It will also involve the discipline to be well prepared for a task and the sensitivity and tenacity to remain flexible and teachable. A change in a personal failure will not happen overnight. There are many times I find myself taking two steps forward and one back. But this is real life. We all suffer; how we suffer can be a testimony for good or whatever we choose. Suffering, defeat, and failure are never welcome or easy to cope with — but they are reality.

How early do people recognize pain? I believe it's when we first begin to walk, and it is a progression until we die.

This poem on the next page was written by my daughter Jennifer when she was thirteen years old. She lost her dad at age five, and she had also experienced the loss of her grandparents and other loved ones. I believe the poem shows that teenagers understand pain and loss.

BEYOND THE PAIN

In a life such as mine, you learn to forgive.

You learn not to hate ones that hated you first.

You help the ones that hurt as you did.

And love others who don't seem to hurt at all.

But even if we don't show how we feel down inside,

We do have wounds in our hearts

But have learned to turn the scars into stars.

By turning those scars into stars,

We have not forgotten what has been done,

But have more than forgiven and tried to go on.

The scars will always be there,

But we can always look toward the future

And realize that the best is yet to come.

In a life where so many loved ones have left you,

It becomes hard to trust...and try to love again.

But by loving and trusting others,

I have learned that there are many people

That have tried to love me, and I have rejected them

As others once rejected me.

But with the love of Christ and loved ones,

I have realized that forgiving is a very precious thing.

Even by looking beyond the pain, hurt, and tears,

I have found that loved ones seem to always help me through.

(Matt. 6:14-15, Col. 4:12-14)

—Jennifer McCullough
June 6, 1990

FINANCIAL FAILURE

On a daily basis, we read the newspapers and magazines and hear the heartbreaking news of so many good people having to declare bankruptcy. What tragedy, pain, and hurt these people are experiencing. The following story, or a variant of it, has been told by many motivational speakers to help put this kind of failure into perspective:

THE RICHEST MAN IN THE VALLEY

A rich landowner named Carl loved to ride his horse Rajah through his vast estate so that he could congratulate himself on his wealth. One day while on such a ride, he came upon Hans, an old tenant farmer, who had sat down to eat his lunch in the shade of a great oak tree.

Hans didn't notice the approaching horseman at first because his head was bowed in prayer. When he did look up, he said, "Oh, excuse me, sir. I didn't see you. I was giving thanks for my food."

"Hmph," snorted Carl, noticing the course dark bread and cheese constituting the old man's lunch. "If that were all I had to eat, I don't think I would feel like giving thanks."

"Oh," replied Hans, "it is quite sufficient. But it is remarkable that you should come by today. Sir, I...I feel I should tell you, I had a dream just before awakening this morning."

"And what did you dream?" Carl asked with an amused smile.

"Well, it wasn't all that clear, sir. You know how dreams are. It seemed there was beauty and peace and music all around, and yet I could hear a voice saying, "The richest man in the valley will die tonight." In fact, that was the one part of the dream that was clear, and I woke with those words on my mind."

By now the amused smile had faded from Carl's face and he was frowning.

"I don't know what it all means, sir," Hans continued. "Perhaps nothing. But I thought I ought to tell you."

"Dreams," snorted the landowner. "Nonsense." And he turned and galloped away.

As Hans watched horse and rider disappear, he prayed, "Lord, have mercy on his soul if he really is to die so soon."

Carl galloped Rajah only a short distance and then slowed the beautiful Arabian to a walk. Die tonight? It was ridiculous, of course. No use his going into a panic. That kind of reaction was what made such predictions come true. If he went galloping like a fool through the forest, he probably would fall and break his neck. The best thing to do about the old man's dream was to forget it.

But he couldn't forget it. Die tonight? How could he, sitting perfectly safe now in his own home? He felt fine. At least, he had felt fine until Hans described his stupid dream. Now he didn't feel too well.

For a while he debated with himself about it, but finally that evening he called his doctor, who was also a personal friend. "Could you come over?" he asked. "I need to talk with you."

A little later, his examination complete, the doctor was full of assurances. "Carl, you're as strong and healthy as that horse of yours. There's no way you're going to die tonight." He chuckled. "Unless you shoot yourself or something like that."

Carl didn't think his friend's remark was terribly funny. "Look," said the doctor, "if it will make you feel any better, I'll be glad to stay a while."

The two friends visited for an hour or so and then played cards through the night. As dawn broke, Carl thanked his friend and told him how foolish he felt for being upset by an old man's dream.

It was about 9 a.m. when a messenger arrived at Carl's door. "It's old Hans," the messenger said. "He died last night in his sleep."

The richest man in the valley had not been the one with the vast holdings, but the man of simple faith in Jesus. It's a story to remember when you think you've lost everything.

I BELIEVE IN MIRACLES

In July, 1989, I spoke to eight hundred sales managers for Home Interiors during their national sales meeting here in Dallas. From noon until 6 p.m. I autographed copies of my book and gave hugs to perhaps 90 percent of these women. To do this for six hours might not seem tiring to some; however, when I did have time to relax, eat a bite, and check my schedule, I discovered that I had promised a small group of retired church librarians I would speak that night at their annual banquet downtown at First Baptist Church.

I went immediately from the sales meeting to the engagement. Two young men from the Zig Ziglar Corporation were kind enough to accompany me — Mike Vander Werf and Scott Tibbels. They graciously handled the driving, parking, and the books, and did everything they could to make me comfortable. We arrived at the banquet just in time for me to speak.

After the banquet, I was relieved to hear Mike say, "Miss Mamie, aren't you hungry?"

Oh, I was! So we stopped in a restaurant on Central Expressway to eat a late-night dinner. I had just taken my first bite when I noticed Mike staring at me. His face had turned white. I asked, "Mike, did you see a ghost?"

"No, Miss Mamie, but the stone from the center of your diamond cluster is gone."

I looked down to see that indeed there was an empty setting where the beautiful two-carat center stone should have been. Where in the world had I lost it? I had been all over Dallas that day and had been so busy I had no idea when it had fallen out. Mike and Scott were visibly shaken. I could only say, "I'm sick, but there is nothing I can do about it now."

By the time I got home, I was so hurt and tired that I went in my back door crying. (You guys know that is what we girls do when we are upset.)

Staying with my children that night was a wonderful friend, Lois Hodges, a very wise lady who kept "prayed up." She looked at me with a loving, caring heart. "Miss Mamie, quit that crying. If God wants you to have that diamond, He'll show you where it is. If not, you don't need it."

I was a little — no, a lot — taken aback. "Lois, don't you understand this is the ring that the children's father gave me in 1971 as an engagement ring? I could never afford another two-carat diamond, and the sentimental value is irreplaceable."

"Straighten up, Miss Mamie," Lois said. "God is in control and He knows what is good for you."

I will not say I went to bed relieved. I did not feel relieved — I felt heartbroken and very lonely at that moment.

The next morning I went to the office, where everyone had heard the news about my ring. I stated that I had not had time to look for it but thought I would find it. I'm sure some of the office crew thought, *It's her age — she doesn't know how hard it is to find a diamond.* However, as time passed, I felt a certain peace about it. My friends asked me about the ring and wondered if I had turned in the report of having lost it to my insurance company. My reply was no, I hadn't had time. I literally had not talked about it in several weeks.

Coming home from church one Sunday, one of my good friends, Herschel Wells, brought up the subject of the diamond. "Herschel," I said, "I feel that the diamond is somewhere very close. I just have not had time to look for it."

He asked, "Have you looked in the car?"

"No."

"Do you want me to help you look for it?"

Of course I replied, "Yes."

He pulled into the grocery store parking lot across from the church. "I'll look in the back seat of the car, and you look in the front," he said.

I got out, pushed the button to move the front seat back, and there in the middle of the floorboard under my front seat was the loose diamond. As I picked it up I said, "Herschel, Lois was right. I turned the diamond deal over to God and in His time He has shown me where the diamond was being kept for me."

Even though my car had been driven by some friends to a funeral in Ohio, to a seminar in Lufkin, Texas, and on many other errands by various people (it also had been cleaned out several times), the diamond had been kept very safe and very near all that time.

Like the diamond, many of our valuables, such as talent, resources, friends, and loved ones, are often close at hand, and we don't even realize it. Until we turn our concerns over to God, things do not always work out.

How long is a lifetime? It is not the distance you travel, but the manner in which you travel that determines how long it is.

When I was growing up in Georgia, I remember thinking that a lifetime was forever, forever, and forever. Why? Because I did not have the knowledge, the maturity, or the understanding to realize that the distance and quality of life depend on my choices. The decisions that I make in my life will ultimately determine my success or failure.

Taking the responsibility for life is awesome — sometimes heavy, sometimes discouraging, but necessary. Dr. Frank Crane would advise patients, "Responsibility is the thing people should dread most of all. Yet it is the one thing in the world that develops us, gives us manhood or womanhood fiber."

Here are some simple steps to take in order to live life to its fullest — with responsibility:

1. Do not cling to your past. Build your life on yesterday's experiences. Profit by your past mistakes and successes, but do not allow them to conquer you. Others may stop you temporarily, but you are the only one who can stop you permanently.

2. Surround yourself with people whom you respect — mentors, friends, colleagues, associates — people who have strengths you hope to acquire and emulate.

3. Be grateful for your material possessions, but do not allow them to possess you. They are to enjoy and share. The only thing on this earth that will live forever is what we do for the Lord and for others.

4. Be honest. Honesty means standing for integrity and for the truth. Speak, walk, and talk honestly. Make this your way of life.

5. Find your talents and use them. Don't worry about something you cannot do, or a special talent or skill you may not have. Find what you can do, and do it with all your might, as positively as you can.

6. Be careful not to pass the buck. Take responsibility for your actions and realize that all actions have consequences for which we are also responsible.

7. Be enthusiastic. If you do your job well, you will enjoy it. But if you do not do it well, you will dislike it. What we do with enthusiasm is usually done well, and how well we do our jobs will depend on our enthusiasm. If you are not enthusiastic about your work, then perhaps you have the wrong job. This is the time to make some changes. First, check your personal life to see if it is the problem. If not, you may have to make a job change. Don't be afraid. It's never too late to *start*.

8. Be consistent in prayer, praying confidently and constantly. Attend a church or synagogue regularly.

9. Be a dreamer. Think big. But be very careful with whom you share your "go-up" or "blow-up" dreams. They are important, though, and we need to keep a record of them on a dream sheet. Challenge others to "dare to dream" too.

GET IT TOGETHER — HERE'S HOW:

1. Remember that failure and a "defeated attitude" are only temporary. They become permanent when we allow them to be permanent — when we quit trying. Only then have we failed.

2. Realize that we all fail at times, but it's how we deal with those events that determines our future. Failure is a reality of life.

3. Take simple, positive, "bite-size" steps to overcome failure.

4. Life is a do-it-yourself kit. Consider how you will put yours together.

5. Keep in mind that most of life's problems can be solved with slight adjustments. We do not necessarily need a complete overhaul.

6. Don't quit trying when the going gets rough. The best fruit grows in the valleys. Working through the hard and difficult times helps us grow and develop character.

7. Dear God: I have a problem, and it's me. Dear Child: I have a solution, and it's Me.

CHAPTER 11

SUCCESS IS A JOINT EFFORT — BUILD YOUR TEAM

A true friend is one who takes you in when the rest of the world has cast you out.

—Anonymous

Few People Are Successful Unless a Lot of Other People Want Them To Be

Geese don't get high-powered press coverage like seagulls. They're seen as dull, ordinary birds that only attract notice twice a year during migration. Like the Blue Angels precision flying team, they fly wing tip to wing tip. You can hear the beat of their wings whistling through the air in unison. And that's the secret of their strength.

Together, cooperating as a flock, geese can fly a 70 percent longer range than when they fly alone. The lead goose cuts a swath through the air resistance, which creates a helping uplift for the two birds behind him. In turn, their beating wings make it easier on the birds behind them, much like the drag of a race car sucked in behind the lead car.

Each bird takes his turn at being the leader. The tired ones fan out to the edge of the V for a breather, and the rested ones surge toward the point of the V to drive the flock onward.

If a goose becomes too exhausted or ill and has to drop out of the flock, it is never abandoned. A stronger member of the flock will follow the failing, weak one to its resting place and wait until it is well enough to fly again.

Geese instinctively help each other. Natural creatures in our universe function and show us mortals the way we should live. They support each other; they are interdependent. This is the type of help, support, and security we need as individuals. Life is not easy, so we need help at every turn in the road. The more people we can enlist to play on our team, the better chance we will have of winning.

There are some small steps you can start taking today that will help you to build this kind of support system. You need to expand your support system by surrounding yourself with the best people you can find. Seek out the smartest, brightest, most talented people available with whom to associate. These kinds of people are successful, and they will make you look good. Where do you look for these people? Go to church, go to education meetings, the Chamber of Commerce, the symphony guild. These are the movers and shakers of the community; they will lend support when you need it. Acquaintances at bars are not the ones to develop.

SUCCESS IS A JOINT EFFORT

We all have the need to be loved and appreciated. That's why so many of us enjoy family reunions, class reunions, college reunions, homecomings, and birthday parties. These are memory-making times when we gather as a group to reminisce and exchange ideas. Rodgers and Hammerstein's lyrics are famous: "Getting to know you, getting to know all about you...."

Our forefathers came over on the *Mayflower;* our grandparents rode across the plains to settle. They all worked very hard during the day but gathered at night, perhaps on the deck of the ship or around the campfire on the prairie to share the day's experiences. In the old movies about crossing the country, you will remember when good or bad times came, the pioneers always shared, sometimes at the watering hole while resting after traveling all day by mule team, sometimes at funerals or at the bedside of the sick. These people were willing to share their ups and downs.

In our present decade we still need this bonding and processing. I believe this is an important part of being a healthy person. Yet many individuals — married, single, divorced, young, old — do not have any significant time with others. Even if today we live in a household with children, statistics show that rarely do we even sit down together for a full meal or share with family members the day's activities, hopes, disappointments, dreams, hurts, and challenges. No wonder we have suicide, depression, drugs, alcoholism, divorce, teenage pregnancy, loneliness, and a hopeless and homeless society. Look around. What do you see? We have to reach out first to those closest to us in our family, and then we have to build a support system to maintain balance and continuity in our lives.

TURTLE ON A FENCE POST

Have you ever driven along a country road? When I was a little girl, during the summer I used to ride down the dusty clay roads of South Georgia. As we went along, I would often see a turtle stranded on top of a fence post. Anytime you see a turtle on a fence post, you will know that he did not get there by himself. There is no way a turtle can climb a fence post.

So it is in building a family, organizing a business, writing a book, or making a speech; it takes a lot of people to make it happen. The point of this story is that the person at the top, heading a family or a corporation, didn't get there by himself or herself; it takes a lot of people to make things happen, and we need to work together to build a better place in which to work and live. We need the help of others, and they need us. Build a support system — get and give help; the principle works both ways.

BEE AN ANGEL!

For many years I have had some special friends with whom I have been very close. Some are in education, some are in the corporate world, some are in direct sales, some are housewives; in fact, there are about twenty females I have been close to for as long as forty-something years. Sometimes we do not talk or visit for long periods of time; however, we always feel bonded in a kind of "soul sister" relationship.

When I turned fifty, some of my friends decided it would be fun to have a big celebration here in Dallas. Friends came from Indiana, Louisiana, Oklahoma, and from all over Texas. They had it planned. I just furnished my home for the meeting place. More than a dozen of them stayed at my home from Friday through Sunday — what a blast! What made it so interesting is that for ten or more years I had talked about them, but most of them had never met each other. When they did all meet, it was "instant" friendship.

What a blessing for me to have so much love, kindness, and friendship in one weekend! While I was preparing for our special time together, I remembered that I had called these friends through the years my Angel Pocket Friends. I had always thought of them as angels. Though I could not always see them, I always knew they were there in my mental pocket. Many times when I have been up late at night working on a project my friend Velma Walker has called me to ask, "Are you all right?" Sometimes I would be; sometimes I needed to talk. An Angel Friend is one who is a messenger from God, and one who is always on your side. We all need Angel Friends from time to time to help prop us up. In fact, I began the Angel Friends' newsletter, *The Encourager,* because I found so many people who need a friend and need encouraging. *Beeing* an angel simply means doing for others, whether they can see you doing it or not. It means being supportive, caring, loving, and understanding.

Who is your hero? Whom do you admire? Your heroes tell a lot about you. If you admire the J. R. Ewings of this world, you are in trouble; yet the TV makes his dishonesty and immoral acts seem glamorous. Although we live in an "I-me-my" world, there are still modern-day heroes who live courageous, worthwhile lives. They trudge uncharted paths through the day-to-day world; they deserve admiration.

In recent years, we have seen some of our heroes crumble. We are all human, with many flaws, of course. But in choosing heroes we still must pick out people whom we can admire, look up to, and emulate. We copy our heroes (or *sheroes*, as the case may be): we imitate how they look, how they act, and how they live. Let's be very careful that our choices are worthy of our trust.

Another word for hero is *mentor*. Mentors may be personal friends or acquaintances — they often are. Other "helpers" may be people you don't even know but whom you admire for their goals, morals, beliefs, personal characteristics, or lifestyles. You may see these people often or infrequently or never at all, but if you share their desires and become better because of them, you are building a firm part of your support system.

I have some mentors who have been on my support team for years, one of whom is the late Mary Crowley — wife, mother, businesswoman, and author who served on many boards across the country. She built her company, Home Interiors, on Christian Biblical principles of honesty, integrity, love, and lots of good common sense. She was dedicated to lifting up others, giving them a plan not only for business, but for life. Her message to all was to serve, and she truly lived and taught this very important principle of life: you reap what you sow.

What an extraordinary woman! I only wish I could have known her before she died. Yet, through her books and the wonderful people at Home Interiors, I feel I do know her. She was truly a godly woman, and I know God, so I feel that gives us a mutual acquaintance and makes us friends.

To carry on her work, she left some very talented, dedicated people whom I have had the opportunity to get to know. These are people who — like Barbara Hammond, the National Sales Manager for Home Interiors for many years — have made an impact on my life. Barbara has the same ideals, love, and commitment to excellence that Mary Crowley had. Mary Crowley's son, Don Carter, and his lovely wife, Linda, are also good role models, sharing their home and helping others.

Some of my other modern-day heroes are Ruth and Bill Singleton, the couple I mentioned earlier who spent fifty-one happy years unselfishly raising seventeen children. I put great emphasis on family nurturing, just as they did. Their example has helped me build a strong family relationship with my own children, although I am a single parent.

Gertrude Palmer is a hero. I have never seen Gertrude, but I know she lives in California, is 105 years old, and has a zest for life that few of us can match. She loves nineteenth-century history and has recently finished a course called "Effective Living for Seniors." She believes in learning something new every day. I believe in that, too.

The Honorable Faith Johnson of Dallas grew up poor, the youngest of thirteen children, in Atlanta, Georgia. She had a dream of getting an education, attending law school, and becoming a judge. Now she is the first black female judge in the state of Texas, presiding over the 363rd District Court. She dared to look for the rainbows and refused to be defeated by poverty and difficult times. She lived on only eight hundred dollars the entire first six months she was in law school. She truly is a person I want to emulate because of her faith and determination to be better. Judge Johnson has lived her life with the ageless four P's principle: Preparation, Persistence, Purpose, and Prayer.

Another of my mentors is my dear friend Rena Tarbet. She is surely someone to capture our fancies and personify our dreams — a real role model. Rena is beautiful, rich, successful, and optimistic. She has everything that anyone could wish for. But Rena also has cancer, and she has been waging the most critical battle of her life. After a radical mastectomy, she endured six years of chemotherapy, but through this courageous struggle she has been a constant inspiration to others. As I told you earlier, Rena put her life in God's hands and prayed for Him to use her — sick or well. Rena's cancer is now in remission, and she is helping hundreds of others who need her example and encouragement. I am proud to say she is a friend — my hero, my mentor, and a member of my team.

Dr. and Mrs. Guy Newman — the epitome of a loving, intelligent and caring couple — believed in me when I could not believe in myself. I shall always cherish the years I lived with them when I was a student

SUCCESS IS A JOINT EFFORT — BUILD YOUR TEAM

at Howard Payne University. They treated me with love and encouraged me beyond belief. Each time I have the opportunity to encourage, share, and support any youth organization, I feel I am repaying the Newmans for their support of me.

Zig and Jean Ziglar have been like family to me since 1974 when I met them at a Mary Kay Cosmetics Seminar in Atlanta, Georgia. Jean is a gracious, loving, kind, and supportive wife and friend to Zig. I appreciate Jean for her role as wife and mother — she has been an inspiration to me and so many others. Zig was the first "motivational speaker" I ever heard. My gratitude and appreciation go to him for his encouragement. Being able to work with him for ten years in his organization was a learning experience and a time of growth for us all.

Perhaps my greatest mentor of all is my mother. Even though Mama had no formal education past the second grade, she was certainly the kind of lady we all love and admire. Her love for her children and her dedication in raising us alone has been an inspiration to many. In the seventy-five years she lived, I do not remember ever hearing her say an unkind remark to or about anyone. She was the first encourager in my life. She never criticized my hair or my dress, or even suggested that she did not like anything about me. She did, however, correct my behavior. She praised and punished with kindness, understanding, and unconditional love. She was perhaps the first true Angel Friend I ever had.

TOGETHER WE CAN

My heart knows and my mind believes that Together We Can
Accomplish anything with strong desire and a proven plan,
Each taking and each giving a helping hand
To achieve worthy goals and thus lift this Land!

We start here, in this place, now,
To persevere and overcome — together we solemnly vow.
The past is rehearsal — it matters not at all;
What counts is today and the future — whatever our call.

Carry our principles high, carry them proud;

Support one another: pass the word — calmly or loud.

We are all in this together to the successful end.

Together We Can catch and ride a winning trend.

And when at last on the high ground victorious we stand,

With circumstance and adversity now under our command,

We shall continue to send to others the simple message again

and again:

Join Together — that's the Key. You can make it!

We did — and — Together You Can!

(Presented to the original Angel Friends, April, 1990)

Broaden your base of support. Widen your circle. The more friends you have and the more people you know, the more support personnel you will have on your team. There should be a group of supporters encouraging you in your family life, another supportive group in your church and spiritual life, and still another group in your career and business life. Go out of your way to make overtures of friendship to any and all whom you think will broaden your horizons and help you to *bee* better.

Opportunities come to you through these people, these acquaintances, these heroes, these mentors, these supporters. Look for the opportunities and seize them. This is more of that positive doing that will help us. No man or woman is an island. We must live for, by, and with others. When we give support, we get support. Build your team!

Even small children build a support system, so it must be instinctive to look for and expect help. (I might add here, if we do not expect things from others, we certainly will not receive them.) Of course, parents and grandparents are always a part of children's support structure, but most children also have inanimate playmates they love and depend on, as if they were real. They have a security blanket or a stuffed animal that they can't sleep without.

Have you ever had to turn over the world looking for that old rabbit, Pooh Bear, or worn-out blanket?

We adults, as well, gather around us inanimate objects with which we are comfortable, things that make us feel secure and happy. Our homes often provide us with a retreat and help in facing the outside world. Our churches are places of refuge (I do not believe that the church as the living Body of Christ is an inanimate object; rather I am speaking of the physical plant itself), and so become part of our support system. My old blue bathrobe or my faded jeans can be comfortable and thus become part of the system.

The more of these comforting items we can gather around us, the broader our base of support.

OUR LIVES ARE TOUCHING

Of things that mean the most
And of things that mean so much
The most meaningful thing is
When lives of friends touch.

For something very special,
Which I cannot define,
Occurred in my living
When your heart touched mine.

Memories of that moment
Now cling without my clutching,
And every day grows sweeter
*Because our lives are touching.**

---

*Perry Tanksley, *Friend Gift* (Old Tappan, NJ: Fleming H. Revell, 1972), p. 12, © 1972 by Perry Tanksley. Used by permission of Perry Tanksley.

GET IT TOGETHER — HERE'S HOW:

1. "We" makes "me" stronger. Let's pull together as a team at home and at work. Remember that "team" has no "I."

2. Remember that success is always a joint effort. We need others to help us build and achieve. No one makes it without others.

3. *Bee* creative.

4. Spend time with people who are for you, not people who are against you.

5. Select your mentors carefully. Choose people you wish to "copy." We become like the people with whom we associate.

Chapter 12

Just Do It!

When I came to Dallas, one of the things I did not tell Mr. Ziglar or anyone else is that I have had problems with claustrophobia since 1976.

How well I remember when it began. I was pregnant with Jennifer and attending a Georgia vocational meeting in Atlanta. My room was on the tenth floor of the Hilton, and in the middle of the night I woke up in a cold sweat; I felt that my skin was crawling and that someone had a big hand around my body, just squeezing and squeezing. I couldn't even breathe. My heart was beating very fast. I got up, dressed, and went down to the lobby — I had to get outside. That was the first attack of claustrophobia that I recall ever having.

Jennifer was born in three weeks, and I remember well how Don had to work to get me a corner room in the hospital so I could see outside and open a window. I continued to struggle with claustrophobia in small, tight places for some time. Eventually I overcame or adjusted to some of the fear, but I still had some of it, too.

I didn't dream when I started traveling for Mr. Ziglar with the Ziglar Corporation that my claustrophobia was going to be a major problem; however, that was the case for several years. I was so embarrassed about the problem that I did not tell anyone.

The first year of the three and one-half to four years that I traveled for the Ziglar Corporation, I accumulated many airline miles going to speaking assignments at schools around the country. The second and third years my travel time was doubled, but I still told no one at the Ziglar Corporation that I had this problem.

When I made these trips, I always requested rooms on the bottom floor. Unless I got a downstairs room where I could open a window, I could not stay in the room at night. Ninety-nine percent of the time, rather than sleeping in the bed, I slept in a chair in the lobby of the hotel. Many nights I tried to go to sleep with the light on, listening to the television or radio, listening to tapes, reading the Bible, or praying. I tried everything, but I simply could not stay in a room with the door shut. Finally, I would go to the lobby. I know I had the Lord's protection because, in all the nights I spent in hotel lobbies, I was never afraid.

When I tell about these experiences, some of my listeners ask how I handled this phobia, trapped in a closed-up airplane while flying to my various speaking engagements. That was a different matter; I had no alternative. When I felt the doors being shut and secured, I knew I could not open the window or the door to relieve my tensions. By gritting my teeth and accepting the reality that this was something I had to do, I put mind over matter. I would busy myself reading, talking to my seat partner, preparing my speech, or eating lunch. It was not easy, but we do what we have to do.

A lot of times we look at our fears and think they cannot be overcome, but I sincerely believe you can overcome them if you face them and *just do it*. Now I travel about 125,000 miles every year and spend a great deal of time in airplanes and hotel rooms, but I have learned to control my claustrophobia. Oh, yes, there are still times when I get really tired and have a little bit of trouble, but not so that I can't rest. It goes back to positive doing; just grit your teeth and do what has to be done.

When I came to Dallas to write the I CAN curriculum and to get I CAN into the schools, I am sure I would not have made the move if I had known that I was suffering from such severe claustrophobia. But I believe when something is right and you know in your heart it is right, the Lord is going to make it right in your head. So I moved to Dallas.

It was my head that was causing the problem. I never really had any professional counseling on this, but I feel that the problem began because of my having been abused as a child. Trying to hide from my abuser, I would get into places that I could not get out of, and I was terribly frightened. I think that my claustrophobia was a sort of flashback to those episodes. I knew that I had to face and erase that memory, because I knew I couldn't do anything about what had happened to me as a child.

When I got pregnant with Jennifer, Brian was still a small child and Patti was only two. I felt again as if I were trapped in a situation I couldn't get out of, so I had to make the best of it. I believe it was the unexpected pregnancy with Jennifer that helped trigger these flashbacks. The situation was serious, and I had to deal with it. I found "Mind Over Emotions," a series of tapes by Dr. Les Carter, a Biblically oriented psychotherapist in Dallas. I kept listening to those tapes and did some of the things he suggested. If I had not been willing to get help, I might still be sleeping in hotel lobbies. Lena Horne has a phrase that I like and have used many times. It keeps me humble, "I've come a long way...maybe?"

We are inclined to let things roll along and not to rock the boat. It is easier not to make a change, but the greatest danger of all is inaction.

TO DO NOTHING

There are several reasons we do nothing:

1. There is a natural resistance to change.

2. We wait around for something to happen.

3. We feel overwhelmed by the situation.

4. It seems to us that the time is not right.

5. There is a lack of confidence that we can improve things.

6. All kinds of adversity keeps getting in the way.

7. We tell ourselves we don't feel like doing anything differently.

The law of mutation teaches us that all things change. We must understand this law and make it work for us. Do not be the first to try something new, but don't be the last to lay the old aside.

We all face some fear when treading on an unfamiliar path, whether it is meeting new friends, moving to a new location, attending a new school, or taking on a new task. As with everything, we must deal with our fears.

Cultivate some phrases which you can readily recall to replace the "fear" words, for example:

FEAR PHRASES	POWER PHRASES
I can't	I'll try
I don't like	It's a learning experience
It's a problem	It's an opportunity
What will I do	I know I can handle it
I'm stuck	I have a responsibility
I'm never satisfied	I want to learn and grow
I'm tired of trying	I know things will change

Keep some positive words handy: *can, try, possible, hope, opportunities, do it.* We are what we put into our minds. Remember what I've said before: *What the mind harbors, the body manifests.* What are we manifesting without words and actions?

Let's quit beating ourselves up mentally by allowing fears to control us and rob us of our talents and abilities.

Zig Ziglar says that *fear* may be interpreted to mean "false evidence appearing real." How many old "fear tapes" do we have in our mental computer banks which are constantly reminding us to fear, fear, fear? Fear immobilizes us mentally and will eventually do the same physically. And, unfortunately, fear is infectious; we can pass it on to others without meaning to.

All you have to do to diminish your fear is to develop more trust in your ability to handle whatever comes your way. Keep affirming: *Whatever happens to me, given any situation, I can handle it.* Naturally, I am taking for granted that the "I" means God and me. God is the God of peace, love, harmony, and contentment. He does not want His children to go through life "scared to death." Remember: God and you are a majority.

Many of us never realize that there are things which will always cause us to be uncomfortable: the dark, death, the unknown. Life will not be easy or without trials and pain — that is a fact of life. However, fear, pain, and troubles should never paralyze us to the point of making us dysfunctional.

Experts generally agree that humans have six basic fears:

1. Poverty

2. Death

3. Ill health

4. Loss of loved ones

5. Old age

6. Responsibility for the future

Then there are reasons why we can't handle these fears:

1. Ignorance of God's Word

2. Selfishness

3. Professional worry syndrome

4. Childhood experiences

5. Negative thinking patterns

And there are strategies to handle fears:

1. Recognize that fear out of context is sin — acknowledge it and confess it to God.

2. Face it; trace it; and erase it.

3. Just do it.

One of my favorite children's books is *The Velveteen Rabbit* by Margery Williams. In this story, two nursery toys, a Rabbit and the Skin Horse, talk about being real.

The Skin Horse was the only toy who was kind to the Rabbit. You see, the Skin Horse had lived in the nursery longer than any of the other toys, and he was very wise.

For a long time the Rabbit lived in the toy cupboard in the nursery. Being made only of velveteen, some of the expensive mechanical toys snubbed him and pretended they were real.

"What is REAL?" asked the Rabbit one day of the Skin Horse. "Does it mean having things that buzz inside you and a stick-out handle?"

"Real isn't how you are made," said the Skin Horse. "It's a thing that happens when a child loves you. It takes a long time. Generally, by the time you are real, most of your hair has been loved off; you get loose in the joints, and you become very shabby."

"Does it hurt?" asked the Rabbit.

"Sometimes," said the Skin Horse. "But when you are Real, you don't mind being hurt."*

As we grow through life, we become real...

...we learn to live

...we learn to accept

...we learn to adjust

...we learn to respond

...we learn to love

...we learn to help

...we learn to encourage

...we learn how to handle hurt and loneliness

...we learn to process hurts and fears

---

*Margery Williams, *The Velveteen Rabbit* (New York: Scholastic, Inc., 1990).

...we learn to *just do it.*

Yes, it would be nice if we could learn these lessons early in life, and some people do. It seems to have taken me a little longer than some, however. Now I try to *bee* "real" — and I don't fear being hurt. As the Velveteen Rabbit story illustrates, we have a responsibility to help others to *bee* "real." Loving and encouraging others makes us develop and grow and mature.

PERSISTENCE PAYS OFF

Mickey Parker is my nephew. He was born in Thomasville, Georgia, in 1963, the fourth child of my sister Mary Lou and her husband, Rudelle Parker. Mickey was taken to the doctor at regular intervals, and the doctor said he was developing normally. Then they began to notice something strange: he fell often and sometimes he would jerk. One day when he was about one year old, Mary Lou and Rudelle were on their way to church with Mickey between them in the front seat, and he started to have a seizure. Realizing there was something wrong, they took Mickey to Albany, Georgia, to be tested by a specialist. The doctor said that there were definitely problems which the child would probably outgrow by the time he was eighteen, but he also warned that the condition could worsen.

Before Mickey started to school, he never went out of the sight of his mother, twenty-four hours a day, because he was scared of the recurring seizures. He was in pain, and Mary Lou couldn't let him ride bicycles, climb trees, or get near water because of the seizures.

When he began the first grade, his seizures got worse. He was taken to a doctor who prescribed four different kinds of medication to be taken twice a day to control the seizures. The interesting part is that when Mickey was tested verbally in the first grade, he was put in the top 10 percent of the class. However, he did not have the muscle control to write, to stay on the line, or to concentrate. His seizures got worse, and he would scream, kick, and beg to go to the doctor. After the sixth grade he was either in school or with his mother, still twenty-four hours a day.

Mary Lou and Rudelle watched their son go through some traumatic childhood growth. They felt as if their hands were tied. They had taken him to the best doctors they could find, and these doctors had said that all they could do was let him grow out of it, possibly by the time he was eighteen. Mary Lou and Rudelle were devoted Christian family people who did the best they could, but there was still no improvement.

Eventually, Rudelle sold his service station, and Mary Lou, for the first time, went to work in a factory so that she could buy groceries. This enabled the parents to help the child around the clock. Rudelle planted a garden, and every minute that summer Mickey was right behind his daddy, whether they were plowing, picking tomatoes, or fishing. Rudelle also bought Mickey a motorcycle.

We thought Rudelle was losing his mind because the child had seizures, and we could just see Mickey having a seizure, running off the road, and getting killed. Then his parents also bought him a horse, and we questioned that also, as we felt that was an unnecessary luxury. Here they were, barely making a living, and Rudelle was spending his money on a horse.

However, we soon found out that he did know what he was doing. Even though Rudelle did not have a college degree in psychology and child development, he certainly had the common sense to help his child. That summer he taught Mickey to ride the motorcycle; he helped his son develop his body by working in the garden; they went fishing; and whatever was done, they did it together — Mickey never left Rudelle's sight.

In September of that year, the doctor couldn't believe what he saw. He said he had never, in all of his years as a pediatrician, seen so much change in one child! He advised Mickey's parents to reduce his medication.

By Christmas 1975, Mickey was completely off all medication and has not had any anti-seizure medication since. He began to learn; he had no more seizures, no more medication; and he finished high school. He took some special-education classes for some of his subjects, but now you would never know by watching him or talking with him that Mickey had not had a normal childhood.

When he finished high school, he went on to vocational school and got some training in mechanics. He dated a girl for five years and eventually married her. Today, he is twenty-six years old, has a lovely wife, and drives a truck two hundred miles a day (things the doctors said he would never be able to do).

See what can be done if you believe?

Just do it.

When you believe in your heart it is right — try it.

Begin with what you know is right. Rudelle and Mary Lou had a desire to help their child; with their strong belief, they did it.

When God puts a desire in our hearts, He will give us a plan to complete it. Just do it!

The only way to get rid of the fear of doing something is to do it!

The only way to feel better about yourself is to do it!

The only way to GROW through life, not just GO through life, is to do it!

The only way to deal with life and its hardships is to do it!

Life is a Do-It-Yourself Project, so just do it....

GET IT TOGETHER — HERE'S HOW:

1. Face your fears. Get help from books, tapes, professionals.

2. Recognize that fear of the unknown will never be comfortable.

3. Remind yourself: *I've come a long way...maybe.*

4. Remember that we become real through love, maturity, and understanding.

CHAPTER 13

I BELIEVE IN YOU

To strive, to seek, to find, and not to yield.
—Alfred Lord Tennyson

In this book I have tried to give you tools for action to help you make your life better. These tools are useless, though, unless you pick them up and use them. And, as it is with all tools, remember they will have to be maintained. Sharpen your ax occasionally by using one of the ideas presented. Perhaps you will use the Heartitudes daily or perhaps you will start encouraging others. However you choose to put these tools to use — just do it!

HEARTITUDE

I believe in you, because God made you. God never made a mistake. My hope and prayer for you is that you get your life together and remember the good times.

I Believe in You!

I have tried to convey in this book my belief about the future for you. I have related some of my life's most precious, as well as hurtful events in order to encourage you. I have fouled up many times — you have fouled up many times — but we all know that problems cannot be drowned in drugs, alcohol, or any other of today's

frequent remedies, for we know problems can all swim. So I encourage you to take each problem and face it (recognize it), trace it (understand it), and erase it (conquer it).

BROKEN RAINBOWS

During a heavy thunderstorm, a young boy on a bicycle was forced to take shelter inside a service station. When the rain subsided, he went out to begin his bicycle ride. As he stood to get on his bicycle, he noticed on the wet pavement the reflected mixture of gasoline, motor oils, and water. In his excitement at seeing all the bright colors on the pavement, he exclaimed, "Look at all those broken rainbows!"

For most of us, the image of broken rainbows is the image of broken dreams and promises. We have all had some of those and will probably have others in our own lifetimes.

It has been said that there are three things that should not be broken — toys, hearts, and promises. Wouldn't life be much easier if that were possible? But life is a reality, and just as there are broken rainbows on the wet pavement, so there are in our lives. Remember, however, that we see these broken rainbows only when we look down; when we look up, up, up, after a refreshing summer storm, we see a complete rainbow, resplendent in the glory of God's Heaven. Yes, that's where we must always look — up.

I want so many things for you! I want you to get your life together, and, yes, remember where you put it. Success is doing your best every day, and you can control this by acting positively every day. I know in my heart that wherever you are in life, you can be better. Just do it! Start. Start today. Encircle yourself with talented, supportive friends who can open your eyes to opportunities that will enable you to be creative and selfless.

Since everything good starts small, take these little steps, these little suggestions — one at a time or all at once. After all, you only need a tune-up! There are so many people out there who are anxious to encourage you. I will help, just as you must learn to pass that help on by encouraging others. You get when you give, making you richer and richer and richer. You can do it! Start. Start today. Life is wonderful; it is worth living; it is super-good and getting better!

Dear reader, with all my heart, I wish you a winning season. I believe in you. This is such an important message for you to understand that I have decided in closing this book to repeat the poem I used to begin it:

I BELIEVE IN YOU

No matter what you've done — I believe in you

No matter what's happened to you — I believe in you

No matter what people say — I believe in you

No matter if you are rich or poor — I believe in you

No matter your age or size — I believe in you

No matter your IQ — I believe in you

No matter where you live — I believe in you

No matter your position or lack of one — I believe in you

No matter, no matter, no matter...

I believe in you!

HEARTITUDE

I Believe  *in*
You!

— ABOUT THE AUTHOR —

Mamie McCullough is one of the country's most popular motivational speakers and authors. She addresses thousands each year through her seminars and keynote engagements: speaking to churches, schools, and businesses. She has written school programs and authored several books.

Mamie worked with Zig Ziglar for ten years as his Director of Education. She shares life-changing principles that are instrumental in providing strategies, ideas, suggestions, insights, and facts on how to be the best you can be. She is an encourager, author, speaker, wife, and mother, and feels her greatest achievement in life was receiving her M.A.M.A. degree.

To receive a free copy of her newsletter, *The Encourager,* or to write the author, address your correspondence to

Mamie McCullough & Associates
PMB 372
305 Spring Creek Village
Dallas, TX 75248

For information regarding Mamie speaking to your organization call:

1-800-255-4226

Additional copies of this book
and other titles by Mamie McCullough
are available from your local bookstore.

Mama's Rules for Livin, Special Gift Edition

Mama's Rules for Livin'

Rules for Success

I Can, You Can Too!

The *I Can!* Curriculum for Schools

♥•♥•♥•♥•♥

HEARTITUDE

I Believe

in

You!

♥•♥•♥•♥•♥